THE
WILLIAM
MORRIS
LIBRARY

THOEMMES

Printed and Bound by
Antony Rowe Ltd., Chippenham, Wiltshire

REFORM AND REVOLUTION

THREE EARLY SOCIALISTS ON THE WAY AHEAD

William Morris
John Carruthers
Fred Henderson

EDITED AND INTRODUCED BY
STEPHEN COLEMAN

THOEMMES PRESS

This edition first published by Thoemmes Press, 1996

Thoemmes Press
11 Great George Street
Bristol BS1 5RR
United Kingdom

ISBN 1 85506 467 7 : Paperback

The William Morris Library Second Series
Six-volume set : Hardback : ISBN 1 85506 456 1

Publisher's Note

The publisher has gone to great lengths to ensure the
quality of this reprint but points out that some
imperfections in the original book may be apparent.

INTRODUCTION

I. *The Historical Context*

An appealing innocence characterized the early British debate about socialism and how to achieve it. That the case for a society based upon common ownership of resources, democratic control of social affairs and production for need rather than profit possessed superior ethical and logical force than any conceivable defence of the capitalist staus quo seemed to require little justification. It was a matter almost beyond dispute that socialism was the better way. The question was how to bring it about in its most uncorrupted form in the most uncompromising manner possible.

Not only in the contributions to the debate about socialist strategy which are reprinted in this volume, but throughout the period of intense radical vivacity which lasted from the mid-1880s to the early 1920s, there existed an almost diametrically contrary ideological outlook to that which pervades late twenieth-century political debate. The intense contemporary suspicion of grand political visions and the rhetoric of fundamental social transformation, accompanied by ideological uncertainties played out through adversarial conflict based more on ritual than principle, leaves politics at the end of this century and millenium looking rather dull and anaemic. For Morris and his comrades politics was about the making of history, by the many and in accordance with an ethical design more ambitious than any yet conceived or attempted. A century later comfort is sought in mistaken sightings of 'The End of History' and the containment of past plans for progress within a realm of proletarian nostalgia on the Left and triumphalist dismissal from the Right of the assumed failure of all attempts at human self-direction. The Left preserves the memory of Morris's socialist vision, bringing it out for occasional celebratory recognition (the respect which Labourism has always shown to long-dead revolutionaries); while the Right, with utter indifference to historical accuracy, lump together Morris, Mao, Attlee and Stalin, as if the very label 'socialist' declares complicity with all of the crimes which have been committed in the name of that doctrine.

So it is necessary to place the debate between socialist reform and socialist revolution within the context of an age in which the anticipation of a better social order to come was unconfused by the subsequent debate about whether it *had* actually come and whether the state-managed regimes purporting to be socialist should be supported, criticized or opposed. Perhaps political innocence can be regarded as a theoretical luxury, available only to those who are in opposition, but from it emerged an imaginativeness about social power which contrasts sharply with the uninspired pragmatism which constitutes so much of contemporary 'political realism'.

In the 1880s socialism was relatively new on the agenda of British politics. Despite his long stay in London, Marx's direct influence in stimulating a socialist movement amongst British workers was slight; although his published writings and the record of his energetic support for trade union internationalism were later to leave their mark. In the year of Marx's death the Democratic Federation, which comprised a network of politically disparate radical workers' clubs, adopted a programme which was essentially socialist and changed its name to the Social Democratic Federation (SDF). One of its most significant new recruits was William Morris who was soon elected to the Executive Council as Treasurer. Already a nationally-known figure as a poet and designer, who had met with considerable political frustration in his earlier collaboration with Liberal politicians and their trade union supporters over the Eastern Question, the energy which Morris brought to Britain's first Marxist party was second to none. He threw himself wholeheartedly into the SDF's work, writing and speaking (in the open air as well as the lecture hall). But from the outset the seeds of dissension between the reformers and the revolutionaries were present.

The root of the dispute concerned the role of a socialist party. Was it to improve or remove capitalism? Those in the SDF who advocated improvement through reform certainly did not argue that palliation was an end in itself, but that socialist-supported reforms would serve as what were called 'Stepping Stones to Socialism'. Marx and Engels, in *The Communist Manifesto* of 1848, had included a list of progressive reforms which would clear the way towards socialism, although in their Preface to the later 1872 edition they withdrew from such advocacy, suggesting that the time for reforming capitalism was past. Morris and a majority of Executive Council members of the SDF took the same view, regarding the task of socialists as being to win workers to an educated support for unadulterated socialism and nothing less. The debate was muddied by the overbearing leadership presence of Henry Myers Hyndman whose commitment to reforms was linked to his conception of himself as a politician and his party as needing to win support on the basis of the kind of paternalistic promises that he thought the workers would be able to understand.

In December 1883 the conflict at the centre of the SDF came to a head. Although Morris and his comrades were in the majority at the Executive Council meeting on the day after Boxing Day when they defeated Hyndman by ten votes to eight, they were the ones to leave the organization. (One wonders what might have happened had they stayed and left Hyndman and his followers to form a splinter party, as indeed they were forced to do in 1916 when the SDF adopted a principled opposition to the imperialist war and the pro-war Hyndmanites formed their own National Socialist Party.)

The split in the SDF cost it some of its finest socialist intellects and activists. As well as Morris there was Eleanor Marx, Edward Aveling and Ernest Belfort Bax. Some two hundred grass-roots members soon went over to the new party, which called itself the Socialist League, for they had not joined a socialist organization to advocate reforms of capitalism. Interestingly, and with an ominous significance, the self-appointed provisional Council of the newly-formed League produced a founding policy statement which, while stating its aim as being 'abolishing the Capitalist and Landlord class', also expressed support

for 'every effort of the wage-earners to win better
conditions of life under the present system' and, in
practical strategic terms which were almost certainly
suggested by Engels, declared specific support for
'Forming...a National and International Socialist
Labour Party; Striving to conquer political power by
promoting the election of Socialists to Local
Governments, School Boards, and other adminis-
trative bodies; [and] Helping Trade-Unionism, Co-
operation, and every genuine movement for the good
of the workers'. The first conference of the League
threw out this statement of policy, regarding it as too
likely to distract strategically from the singular task of
'educating' and 'making socialists'. The League's
Manifesto, adopted at its First Conference in July
1885, was arguably the most articulate and
convincing expression of what has been called
'socialist purism' to come out of the socialist
movement. Unlike the provisional policy statement
drafted by the inaugural Council, the *Manifesto*
rejected 'mere politics' as well as limited schemes for
land nationalization (Henry George's ideas were much
in the air at the time), Co-operation (which it
regarded as being 'competitive co-operation for
profit') as well as what it called 'State Socialism' (a
remarkable anticipation of later critiques of what has
more accurately been labelled as state capitalism).
The *Manifesto* was written by Morris and Bax and
represented an important policy demarcation between
the League and the SDF, asserting for the former the
high ground of socialist politics away from the
combat of would-be parliamentary factions.

The early days of the League were relatively
encouraging: within a year the small membership had

more than doubled. Such unity was not to last for
long. In the general election of 1886 (the first since
the 1884 Act granting majority *male* franchise) the
League issued a leaflet urging workers not to vote, on
the grounds that a diminishing number of voters
combined with a growth in the socialist movement
would frighten the ruling class. To some members of
the League, encouraged by Engels, this position
seemed pointless. After all, had not Marx regarded
the British workers' campaign for the vote as a most
impressive starting point for revolutionary struggle,
and had he not urged the French workers to convert
the franchise from 'an instrument of trickery to an
agent of emancipation'? It seemed to such socialists
that the vote should now be utilized, either in support
of candidates put up by the League itself or to back
the creation of a new party of labour. Morris's view
that all electoral activity would involve collaboration
with the existing system, including its factional
intrigues and corruption, was given greater credence
by the exposure of the deplorable behaviour of the
SDF in the 1886 campaign, which put up two
candidates who were financed by Tory gold: this was
Hyndman's attempt to use the Tories to threaten the
Radical Liberals so that they would accept SDF
reform pressure for the eight-hour day, while the
Tories used the SDF to take away radical votes from
the Liberals. (In the event the SDF candidates only
won fifty-nine votes between the two of them: hardly
a threat to the Liberals or a good investment for the
Tories or any gain worthy of such an abandonment of
principles by the SDF.) Morris was of the view that
such political chicanery was inevitable as soon as one
entered the electoral contest. Others disagreed; at the

League's Second Conference in July 1886 an effort to
change the constitution of the League so as to include
electoral action was roundly defeated, leading the
ever-optimistic Morris to write to his wife that 'the
alterers were defeated and bore their defeat with good
temper'. Two months later Joseph Lane, one of the
more anarchistically inclined East End members of the
League's Council, was provoked to move a motion
complaining that 'some speakers of the League are in
the habit of advocating Parliamentary action and
palliatives of the present system as a means of
bringing about socialism'. From the other side, the
League's journal, *Commonweal*, lost two fine editors
consecutively – first Aveling and then Bax – on the
grounds that they wanted to endorse some degree of
electoral activity. Aveling, with the backing of Engels
whose role as the movement's oracular elder
statesmen until his death two years before Morris's
cannot be overestimated, established what was
effectively an internal faction of the pro-parliamentary
members from mid-1886 onwards. Torn by
principled dissension, in November 1886 the League's
Council adopted the conventional, but so frequently
futile course in leftist circles, of establishing a
committee to consider the question of parliamentary
action and report on a policy that could be agreed by
everyone. The committee linked the parliamentary
question to what it regarded as an inseparable policy
issue of whether the League should support reform
agitation. The assumed inseparability between using
the ballot box as an indication of socialist strength
and using election campaigns as platforms to promote
palliatives was based upon a logical flaw: it is
conceivable that socialists could have put up candi-

dates in elections on a purely socialist manifesto, without reform demands, just as it would have been conceivable for them not to enter elections but still offer support for some reforms. The premise that there is an inevitable link between parliamentary action and reform demands served to confuse the debate. In fact, as we shall see, Morris would have been reasonably content with the former position, but was convinced that any concession to parliamentary action would be a concession to reformism.

The Third Annual Conference of the League in May 1887 considered the report of the committee on parliamentary action which was of little use, for the divisions within the committee had been even more confusing than those within the wider organization. Originally, Binning and Bax were appointed to represent the pro-parliamentary position, while Lane and Mahon were to defend the existing policy. In the course of the committee's deliberations Mahon moved his position (which is hardly a crime given that the object was to reach some agreement), leaving Lane isolated in firm hostility to any form of parliamentary or electoral action. Lane took his minority report, *The Anti-statist Communist Manifesto*, to the Council and asked for it to be issued to the 1887 Conference as a proposed policy. It was rejected, with Morris voting against its anarchist position that the state itself, rather than the state as a means of minority class domination, was the root of oppression. The policy motions put before the Third Annual Conference reflected the deep and probably unbridgeable divisions in the League. Croydon branch proposed an amendment to the constitution stating that socialism should be fought for 'by every available means, Parliamentary or otherwise'. Hammersmith branch, of which Morris was a member, proposed a moderating motion accepting that there were differences over parliamentary action, emphasizing that the League's main task was 'steadily educating the people in the principles of Socialism' and suggesting that the parliamentary question be deferred for a year. Morris seemed at this point to have accepted the view that making new socialists was rather more important than arguing about what would happen once millions were committed socialists. Glasgow branch tabled a resolutely anti-parliamentary motion. (This was opposed by Morris, incidentally, indicating that he was by no means wedded to a dogmatic anti-parliamentary position.) At the conference policy options were confused further by a motion from J. L. Mahon; having originally taken an anti-parliamentary stand on the committee, he now argued that all efforts should be made 'to penetrate the existing political organisations with Socialism'; and that parliamentary and local elections should be used 'for spreading the principles of Socialism and organising the people into a Socialist Labour Party'. Defeated by an anti-parliamentary amendment moved by Morris, the pro-parliamentary group refused to stand for election to the League's Council. This was the beginning of the end for the League, with the pro-parliamentaries intensifying their own faction, led by Aveling and the Scottish lawyer, Donald (both of whom Morris disliked politically and personally), while Morris himself used the League's journal, *Commonweal*, to launch a stinging assault upon so-called 'practical' socialists who seek gradual change and dare not tell voters what socialism means

lest they be regarded as 'unpractical and utopian'.[1] At
the Fourth Annual Conference in 1888 the anti-parliamentary position was confirmed, with the suspension
of the eighty-strong Bloomsbury branch which had
contested seats locally in collaboration with the SDF
for the Board of Guardians. The pro-parliamentary
members, including Eleanor Marx and Aveling,
abandoned the League, first to form the Bloomsbury
Socialist Society and then to return to the SDF.
Morris found himself left within a shrinking organization in the uncomfortable company of a growing
number of anarchists who, having won the day in
opposition to parliamentary action, proceeded to
destroy the League with rhetoric of insurrectionary
adventurism which Morris found even more contrary
to his commitment to education for democratic
socialist change than was the pro-parliamentary
policy. Morris had no option than to retreat from the
League into educative work in his branch which, as
the gulf between it and the mainly East London
anarchists widened, seceded from the League to
become the Hammersmith Socialist Society. In his last
years Morris rejoined the SDF, but with no
enthusiasm at all for its tendency towards adulterated
socialism. Writing in November 1890, Morris
persisted in his opposition both to reformism ('Men
believe that they can wrest from the capitalists some
portion of their privileged profits.... That it could
only very partially be done, and that the men could
not rest there if it were done, we Socialists know very
well; but others do not') and to 'State Socialism' to

---

[1] William Morris, 'On Some "Practical" Socialists', *Commonweal*, vol. 4,
18 Feb. 1888, pp. 52–3.

which he still could not commit himself, but concluded reluctantly that maybe this was a transitional stage on the path to actual socialism.[2]

The early history of the socialist movement in Britain can be examined in two ways: on one level it was an active campaign by men and (some) women, workers as well as others, from small parties, sects and none at all, to introduce into the class conflict which pervaded British politics a sense of class-consciousness and a vision of an alternative way of organizing society. In the heat of activity nuances of theoretical distinction melted and remarkable alliances of conspicuously varying socialists, radicals and anarchists were forged. The battle for free speech on the streets of London was one such occasion for common action; the unprecedented strike for the dockers' tanner was another one. Innocent observers have sometimes sought to confine socialist history to such moments of explicit solidarity, expressing naive hope that it can outweigh those issues upon which socialists have debated and feuded for decades. But these discussions of principle, which are so crucial to the intellectual democracy of a movement characterized by a wish for people to free themselves, are in no way to be regarded as secondary, timewasting or intrinsically doctrinaire. Without them socialist thought could well have become a mere repetition of brave moral sentiments and fighting rhetoric – or worse still, what passes as socialist thought could simply become a coded policy for the more efficient management of capitalism (as some believe is largely the case today). So the policy declarations and

---

[2] William Morris, 'Where Are We Now?', *Commonweal*, vol. 6, 15 Nov. 1890, pp. 361–2.

polemics which have sustained as well as negotiated
the meaning of the socialist idea are as much and as
vital a part of the movement's history as is the record
of victory and failure, bravery and betrayal in the field
of practical action.

It was in the midst of the Socialist League's debate
about parliamentary action that Morris first gave his
lecture on *The Policy of Abstention*. Contrasted with
the policies of his opponents who sought to use
elections as a battleground for winning reforms of
capitalism, and of those anarchists who seemed to
think that the state was best ignored in the hope that
it would go away or be blown up, Morris addressed
the practical question of the means by which socialism
might be established without either becoming
compromised or crushed in the process. *The Policy of
Abstention*, first read by Morris to a Hammersmith
branch meeting on 31 July 1887, and subsequently
repeated before audiences many times, should not be
considered solely within the context of the internal
politics of the relatively small and only modestly
significant Socialist League. Its main political value
lies in its strategic approach to transforming a society
which is dominated by the ethos of parliamentary
gradualism. It should be seen in the context of an
anti-parliamentarist tradition within which emerged
council communism, the strategy of soviet power, and
syndicalism.

The name of John Carruthers is little known in
books on the development of socialist thought,
although his own contribution both to Morris's
socialist convictions and to the debate about the value
of reformist politics has been immensely underes-
timated. As an influence upon Morris, we know that

Carruthers was with him in the Society for the Protection of Ancient Buildings and that his acceptance of Marxian economic theory (or a slight variant of it, at least) pre-dated Morris's. In 1883 he published his refutation of the classical theories of Mill and Ricardo, *Communal and Commercial Economy*, and not long after that his name appears on the minutes of the Hammersmith branch of the League in which he remained into the following decade as a member of the Hammersmith Socialist Society, lecturing for it in Morris's last years with a persistent commitment to the integrity of a revolutionary rather than palliating position. If Bax is to be credited with influencing Morris above all on matters of Marxian economics and philosophy (and doubts could be entertained about Bax's fitness for this role),[3] Carruthers more than any other sustained Morris in his strategic outlook, never wavering on the question of reformism. His pamphlet, *Socialism and Radicalism*, published by the Hammersmith Socialist Society in 1894 (precisely when Morris was trying to persuade himself of the possible necessity of 'state socialism') was not only, as E. P. Thompson rightly observed, 'a masterly exposure' of state ownership and limited reform demands, but must have helped to keep such a critique alive at a time when, with the emergence of the Independent Labour Party as a popular body confining itself to policies of trade union-based reforms, it would have been quite possible for the 'purist' position to be forgotten as an obsolete irrelevance. Carruthers' experience as a structural engineer, with working experience in

---

[3] See John Cowley, *E. Belfort Bax: A Victorian Encounter With Marx* (London, 1994) and my review of it in the Autumn 1994 issue of *The Journal of The William Morris Society*.

Venezuela and Argentina as well as Australia and
New Zealand, provided him with two qualities.
Firstly, his was the mind of a practical scientist
concerned with precision and the necessity of
transparency between theory and practice. It seems
that the sometimes dour Scottish engineer brought the
consistency of thought so essential when designing
bridges and water supplies to his thinking about
socialist strategy. The result was rarely as strong on
passion as Morris's most stimulating expositions, but
played an immeasurable role in keeping the issues
straight. Secondly, Carruthers' experiences in New
Zealand were particularly important; here was a
country in which many of the plans advocated by
British advocates of state nationalization had been
implemented and if it could be shown, as Carruthers
thought it could, that changes in the form of property
ownership failed to alter the fundamental relationship
between wage labour and capital, this was surely
empirical support of the utmost significance for the
original Morris position. No work written by
Carruthers has been republished since his death, and
the pamphlet herein, contained in the collection of
bound Hammersmith Socialist Society pamphlets in
the Marx Memorial Library (whose kind permission
to reproduce it is acknowledged with gratitude) is an
opportunity to encounter a critique of nationalization
produced half a century before the election of the
post-war Labour government, but much of which
could serve well as a perceptive study of the
limitations of state-run enterprises in the twentieth
century.

Carruthers wrote at a time when the banner of
socialism in Britain was passing from the small
Marxist groups to a wider, less theoretically defined

party, the ILP. Coterminous with the ILP's formation in January 1893 Morris sought to use the small Hammersmith Socialist Society to approach the SDF and the Fabians to form a united Socialist Federation. The result of this move, intended by Morris to pursue unity on the basis of at least some common socialist principles, was *The Manifesto of English Socialists*, issued in May 1893, committing the signatories from all three organizations to agreement on one aim: 'to obtain for the whole community complete ownership and control of the means of transport, the means of manufacture, the mines, and the land. Thus we look to put an end for ever to the wage-system, to sweep away all distinctions of class, and eventually to establish...international communism....' Compared with the markedly unrevolutionary political vocabulary employed by the new ILP (which declined to call itself a socialist party for fear of scaring off moderate support) there were grounds for regarding the *Manifesto* as a means of sustaining a revolutionary socialist voice in British politics, but this was largely an illusory perception. In reality, the *Manifesto* reflected less a collectivity of voices than a paper commitment by prominent intellectuals; the real thunder in 1893 was coming from the north of Britain southwards, not from Morris or Hyndman, but from the ILP which from the start saw itself as an electoral party with no misgivings about the advocacy of a capitalist reform programme.

It is a matter of some curiosity that the ILP at the beginning of the twentieth century decided to adopt Fred Henderson's pamphlet, *The ABC of Socialism*, as its agreed statement of the socialist position.[4] As is

---

[4] See Fred Henderson, *The Case For Socialism* (London, 1911); the preface explains the adoption of *The ABC of Socialism* by the ILP, and the piece constitutes the opening chapter.

clear from reading it, Henderson's analysis is markedly influenced by Morris's anti-reformist stance: hardly a surprising fact given that Henderson joined the Socialist League as a young man and learnt his socialism more from Morris than from Hardie. As a teenager Henderson wrote to Morris asking for advice on writing poetry for the cause of socialism. Morris's letter of advice to the young worker-poet is an interesting indication of his thoughts about the techniques of poetry-writing; at the age of sixteen Fred Henderson published the first of his three volumes of socialist verse.[5] At nineteen, having graduated from Owen's College in Manchester (which later became the University), where he had been politically active, Henderson returned to his native Norwich where he became a founder member of a Socialist League branch, speaking in the open air and embarking on long journeys into rural areas. In 1887 he was arrested and imprisoned in Norwich Castle for exercising his free speech in addressing the unemployed. Norwich soon became the League's most active non-northern branch outside of London. Henderson seems for a while to have tended towards an anarchistic position, leading ironically to a charge being raised against him by Charles Mowbray who was later to become a key figure in the League's absorption into anarchist adventurism. Meanwhile Henderson moved the other way, finding himself increasingly drawn to John Mahon's call for a socialist labour party which could have a real electoral force. In pursuit of such a parliamentary strategy Henderson formed the Clapham Labour

[6] *Echoes of the Coming Day: Socialist Songs and Rhymes* (Norwich, 1887).

League and in 1892, at the age of twenty-four, he was one of the first socialists elected, as a member for Clapham, on to the London County Council. As an ILPer he maintained his basically revolutionary outlook, putting the view against the effectiveness of reform politics as late as 1939 when he was elected as Lord Mayor of Norwich.

Not only is *The ABC of Socialism* a fine example of Morris's approach to reform politics, but it serves to show that the ideas were bigger than the man: that after Morris's death and the demise of any party influenced principally by him his contribution was still present. As Martin Crick has shown in his account of the ILP's early years and strategies for socialist unity, there were indeed forces in the ILP of the 1890s, more on the ground than in the leadership, which did seek federation with the Marxist groups.[6] Indeed, a referendum of 1895 showed a vote within the ILP in favour of precisely such a course of action, but it was ignored by Keir Hardie and his fellow leaders who feared that unity with the SDF, of which Morris was again by then a member, would damage the party's appearance of respectability. The history of unforged coalitions makes for fascinating speculation if little else, but it is worth considering how different the development of labour politics in Britain might have been had it embraced at the outset a Marxist tendency. As it happens, the ILP evolved as a reasonably libertarian organization, allowing mavericks like Henderson to express their own views with impunity.

[6] Martin Crick, '"A Call To Arms": the struggle for Socialist Unity in Britain, 1883–1914', in D. James, T. Jowitt and K. Laybourn (eds.), *The Centennial History of the Independent Labour Party* (Halifax, 1992), pp. 181–205.

On the level of theory, one can see that although the Henderson statement follows closely Morris's repudiation of the reformist policy, it deviates somewhat from orthodox Marxian economics, at least semantically, in its emphasis upon distribution as the key to economic power. In fact, read in accordance with its own logic, Henderson clearly regarded distribution to embrace production and was probably in accord with the Marxist emphasis upon the ownership and control of production as the source of social power. (Marx argued that profit was produced at the point of production and was only realized at the point of sale, so rejecting the argument later put within the ILP and other non-Marxist bodies that the key reform concerned the introduction of fairness into distribution, assuming that profits came about because of unscrupulous overpricing at the point of sale.)

II. *The Argument About Gradualism*

It would be a mistake to see the development of political ideas by Morris and his associates within a vacuum of British radicalism. The debate about the strategy for achieving socialism was remarkably universal in the last two decades of the nineteenth century, with virtually identical positions and splits occurring in countries which had little or no knowledge of the events going on elsewhere.

The Second International, formed in 1889 (the centenary of the French Revolution), served to reflect the universality of these apparently specific and personalized disputes amongst socialists. At its very inception, announced in *Commonweal* on 25 May 1889, there was not one International but two: a possibilist one, in which Marxian theory and revolutionary strategy was not emphasized, and an impossibilist one for the avowedly Marxist parties and groups. Morris attended as a delegate to the latter conference which was held at the same time and in the same city (Paris) as the first. The possibilist-impossibilist split is of no small relevance to the debate between parliament and its opponents, and reform versus revolution. The conflict first became explicit amongst the French socialists after the election of October 1881 in which the Fédération du Parti des Travailleurs, which stood on a revolutionary manifesto, won no more than 60,000 out of the seven million votes cast. This led critics within the Federation, notably Paul Brousse and Benôit Malon, to reject its uncompromising revolutionism, stating that 'We prefer to abandon the "all-at-once" tactics practised until now.... We desire to divide our ideal ends into several gradual stages, to make many of our demands immediate ones and hence possible of realisation.'[7] This emphasis upon the politically possible gave rise to a new label and thereafter French socialists became known as either possibilists or impossibilists, with Jules Guesde and Paul Lafargue as the most prominent advocates of the latter position. In mid-July 1889 the impossibilist International was held in the Salle des Fantaisies Parisiennes (a venue selected with no apparent irony intended), while the smaller possibilist International, attended by British delegates from various trades councils, the TUC Parliamentary Committee and the Fabian Society, met at 10 rue de Lancry. As well as Morris, who reported to the conference on behalf of 'the British socialist

---

[7] *Proletaire*, 19 November, 1881.

movement', there were six other delegates from the
Socialist League, and also several delegates from
Socialist Societies and Keir Hardie representing the
Ayrshire miners. Overwhelmingly representative of
French revolutionary socialists who would permit no
compromise with their possibilist rivals, Morris must
have felt quite at home.

In other countries the same divisions had taken
place. For example, the Socialist Labor Party in the
United States was under the immense theoretical
influence of Daniel De Leon whose political similarity
to Morris deserves closer study, for despite never
meeting one another their socialist temperaments and
strategies had much in common.[8] De Leon was not at
the 1889 congress (the SLP was represented by Busche
and Miller) and was not to attend until 1893 by
which time Morris was not a delegate. In 1899 the
SLP split, with the gradualist minority, known as the
'kangaroos', forming what was later to become the
Socialist Party of America: the party of Eugene Debs.
De Leon, rejecting the value of a reform programme
for a socialist party, persuaded the SLP to adopt a
manifesto with no minimum demands, but only the
single maximum demand of socialist transformation.
Similar positions were taken by impossibilist groups
elsewhere: the Bulgarian 'Narrow' socialists; the
Socialist Party of Canada; the Socialist Party of Great
Britain after its split from the SDF in June 1904. So,
far from being the eccentric position of a utopian
dreamer, we can place Morris's position, and the
others published here, within an anti-gradualist
tradition which was clearly greater than the man or
his immediate political environment.

[8] See Stephen Coleman, *Daniel De Leon* (Manchester University Press,
1991), esp. chap. 6, 'The Case Against Reformism'.

What were Morris's objections to reforms – or palliatives, as he more commonly called them? Firstly, he feared that attempts to alter but a part of the profit system would always be overwhelmed by the ferocity of the whole; a later critic of such a strategy was to compare it to trying to attack a tiger one claw at a time. Two statements by Morris sum up this concern:

> Those who think they can deal with our present system in this piecemeal way very much underrate the tremendous organization under which we live, and which appoints to each of us his place, and if we do not change to fit it, grinds us down until we do. Nothing but a tremendous force can deal with this force.[9]

> The palliatives over which many worthy people are busying themselves now are useless: because they are but unorganized partial revolts against a vast wide-spreading grasping organization which will, with the unconscious instinct of a plant, meet every attempt at bettering the condition of the people with an attack on a fresh side....[10]

Secondly, Morris feared that reforms may very well improve the lot of a section of the working class, perhaps even lifting them by means of welfare support to a condition of imagined release from poverty, but such a situation would serve to divide workers and make them easier to rule; so he warned a correspondent to *Commonweal*, one R. F. E. Willis 'whither the whole system of palliation tends –

[9] William Morris, 'Art and Socialism', *Collected Works*, vol. 23, p. 208.

[10] William Morris, 'Whigs, Democrats and Socialists', in *Signs of Change: Seven Lectures* (London, 1888, p. 41; 1915 ed., p. 33, repr. Bristol: Thoemmes Press, 1994).

namely, towards the creation of a new middle class to act as a buffer between the proletariat and their direct and obvious masters; the only hope of the bourgeois for retarding the advance of Socialism lies in this device'.[11]

A third objection to reformism rested upon an objection to the perception of socialism as a merely economic change. Morris especially castigated Sidney Webb and the mechanically-reforming Fabians for projects of this kind. The detestation of a formally altered capitalist system, with mechanisms of state control masking the essential continuity of the exploitative and unattractive tensions of the relationship between wage labour and capital, led Morris to an extreme position of preferring to see the nihilistic image of a collapsed property-civilization, brought to ruin by its own inherent chaos, than a vision of well-managed class society: municipally-regulated poverty.

What are we to make of these objections to reformism a century after they were stated? To be sure, it has been a century in which reforms of every kind by parties of every colour have been enacted, both in national parliaments and by local authorities. The first objection could, on the face of it, be seen to have been rather too precious in its theoretical dismissal of 'something now'. After all, if the capitalist beast is always stronger than the taming inclination of reformers, how ever would changes such as the National Health Service or old-age pensions or greater equality for women have come about? To which one might respond that what capital

---

[11] William Morris, 'Socialism and Politics (An Answer To "Another View")', *Commonweal*, vol. 1, July 1885 (Supplement), p. 6.

concedes with one hand it has the power to withdraw with the other when demands of profitability dictate; the gradualism of the late twentieth century tends more towards the erosion of welfare and employment rights than the consolidation of existing ones or the creation of new ones.

As for the fears regarding a new middle class, the experience of the consumer society, culminating in the voracious greed for material possessions fostered by Thatcherism, has led critics such as Jeremy Seabrook to take seriously the dangers of buying off the working class with Ford cars and video machines.[12] The emergence of the one third–two thirds strategy in the advanced industrialized countries (and in another sense, globally), whereby just enough voters are bribed into contentment to secure their indifference to those with little or nothing at all, has proved to be politically successful, but socially divisive and ethically brutalizing.

As for the third objection, here the Morris position may be most enthusiastically attacked and most strongly defended. The attack would be directed at a certain kind of all-or-nothing perfectionism regarded as incompatible with the pragmatic requirements of practical politics. Morris would have been the first to declare his temperamental dislike for the ethical pragmatism of 'practical' politics, although critics could respond that such was the position of an aesthete rather than a revolutionary – and one who was rich enough to wait for the best of times, while others needed to be in more of a hurry. When Carruthers asks why accept crumbs rather than the

---

[12] Trevor Blackwell and Jeremy Seabrook, *A World Still To Win: The Reconstruction of the Post-War Working Class* (London, 1985).

whole loaf, critics might well answer that crumbs are worth a good deal more to a person who is starving than the dream of a whole loaf of bread. The link between remote, futuristic utopianism and a tendency to become detached from the immediacy of human need and despair could engender a callous indifference to present suffering, although this is by no means an inevitable reaction and would not apply to the writers published in this volume. There is an equal reality in the opposite danger: to become so immersed in the expediencies of immediate palliation that one loses sight of any end other than a patched-up present. Overwhelmed by the effects of a malignant social order the reformer could lose sight of the cause, even becoming indifferent to its existence as long as the severity of the ill effects can be contained. The sacrifice of social vision is made for the sake of temporary concessions within what becomes an everlasting 'meantime'. A temptation even to regard basic economic advances within capitalism as socialism itself, leaving the socialist alternative somewhat hollow and meaningless in its alleged realization, is what the anti-reformist socialists sought to avoid. Surely the experience of the various 'socialist' governments, states and policies for capitalism in the twentieth century have given more than a little credence to that concern.

III. *As To Parliament*
Having travelled through the reconstructed and revived London of Morris's utopian romance, and passed along his way the old Houses of Parliament which had now been turned into a storage place for manure, the Guest in *News From Nowhere* settles

down to his meeting with Old Hammond who answers his questions about the arrangements of the new socialist society:

'What kind of government have you? Has republicanism finally triumphed? or have you come to a mere dictatorship, which some persons in the nineteenth century used to prophecy as the ultimate outcome of democracy? Indeed, this last question does not seem so very unreasonable, since you have turned your Parliament House into a dung-market. Or where do you house your present Parliament?'

The old man answered my smile with a hearty laugh, and said, 'Well, well, dung is not the worst kind of corruption; fertility may come of that, whereas more dearth came from the other kind, of which those walls once held the great supporters. Now, dear guest, let me tell you that our present parliament would be hard to house in one place, because the whole people is our parliament...we have no longer anything which you, a native of another planet, would call a government.'[13]

With the public credibility of parliamentarians at an all-time low a century after that was published, there is a contemporary appeal in Morris's vision. What might have seemed wildly utopian and unpractically anarchistic in 1890 these days finds support from those who would remove from constitutionalism the notion of a single decision-making institution and use modern communications technology to wholly decentralize power. From concepts of 'deliberative

---

[13] William Morris, *News From Nowhere*, in Clive Wilmer (ed.), *News From Nowhere and Other Writings* (Penguin, 1993), p. 107.

polling' to 'electric democracy' to 'teledemocracy' to grand claims for the democratizing potential of the Internet, a growing tendency towards regarding Parliament or Congress as the sovereign body is emerging.[14]

Those who study parliamentary democracy write with diminishing confidence about the compatibility of the two concepts. The limited power of parliament over government has long been acknowledged; Lloyd George, addressing the Select Committee on Procedure in 1931 asserted that 'The fact of the matter is that the House of Commons has no real effective or continuous control over the actions of the Executive' and few political leaders since then would disagree very much with him. Squeezed evermore by the powers of corporate interests, unelected governmental bodies, judicial reviews and supra-national sovereignty residing in mainly unaccountable European institutions, and overwhelmed by a degree of information far beyond the purview of any one or committee of MPs, the assumptions underlying parliamentary sovereignty are weakening rapidly. For Morris the power of parliament stood in stark contradistinction to the pursuit of real democracy. Placing into the mouth of Hammond his real views, he asked rhetorically, 'Was not the Parliament on the one side a kind of watch-committee sitting to see that the interests of the Upper Classes took no hurt; and on the other side a sort of blind to delude the people into supposing that they had some share in the management of their own affairs?'[15]   In this assess-

---

[14] See F. Christopher Arterton, *Teledemocracy: Can Technology Protect Democracy?* (Newberry Park, Calif., 1987) and James S. Fishkin, *Democracy and Deliberation* (Yale University Press, 1991).

[15] William Morris, *News From Nowhere, op. cit.*, p. 108.

ment Hammond/Morris was supported towards the
end of the twentieth century by no less an esteemed
political theorist than Ralph Miliband who, writing of
the adoption of democratic rhetoric as part of 'the
common coinage of political speech' after the passage
of the Second Reform Act, observed that

> Earlier generations had feared democracy: their
> successors now proclaimed that it had arrived.
> Whether the people wanted power or not, they now
> had it. The point was to keep the power in safe
> hands while proclaiming that it had passed into the
> hands of the people. If democracy had arrived,
> there was no need to agitate for it.
>
> The politicians' appropriation of 'democracy' did
> not signify their conversion to it: it was rather an
> attempt to exorcize its effects. In reality, the idea of
> democracy had made little progress with
> 'responsible' people. They were reconciled to more
> and more members of the working class having the
> vote ...But they thought it absurd and intolerable
> that ignorant multitudes, quite likely swayed by
> unprincipled and self-seeking demagogues, should
> have real power in the making of policy. A carefully
> limited and suitably controlled measure of
> 'democracy' was acceptable, and even from some
> aspects desirable. But anything beyond that was
> not.
>
> The whole political system was geared to such
> sentiments; and it has remained much more closely
> geared to them than political rhetoric would make it
> appear.[16]

Miliband's Marxist analysis of parliamentarism
essentially reflected Morris's and accounts for the

[16] Ralph Miliband, *Capitalist Democracy in Britain* (Oxford, 1982),
pp. 27–8.

latter's support for absentionism. If parliament existed to manage capitalism inevitably against the interests of the working class, why should the working class support such a machinery of oppression by voting? This was the rationale for the 1886 Socialist League leaflet urging workers to make their mark by not voting, and this was the basis of Morris's consistent antipathy to electoral politics, even though his very last years witnessed some mellowing with regard to what he saw as the progressive reflection of growing class consciousness in the election of workers' representatives to the LCC and other municipal bodies. Others on the Left had a far more sanguine view of the utility of parliamentary democracy in the struggle for socialism; for example, a Fabian tract published in the year of Morris's death declared that 'since England now possesses an elaborate democratic State machinery, graduated from the Parish Council or Vestry up to the central Parliament, and elected under a franchise which enables the working-class vote to overwhelm all others, the opposition which exists in the Continental monarchies between the State and the people does not hamper English Socialists'.[17] This claim, and Morris's counter-claim, give rise to two questions: is 'constitutional democracy' so inseparably linked to minority coercion that it is useless from the standpoint of social democracy? And what are the alternatives offered by those who reject parliament?

There were those who held that parliament could only ever be an enemy of democracy: Joseph Lane, as the most articulate of the League's anarchists was one, and the maverick Guy Aldred (who actually stood

---

[17] Quoted in *ibid.*, p. 23.

more than once as a parliamentary candidate!)
typified anti-parliamentarism in the twentieth
century.[18] But Morris did not belong to this category
of inflexible opponents of the parliamentary ballot
box. Shortly before addressing *The Policy of
Abstention* to the Hammersmith branch, Morris had
written to John Bruce Glasier in Glasgow that 'We
might for some definite purpose be forced to send
members to Parliament *as rebels*...but under no
circumstances to help carry on their government of
the country';[19] in short, the possibility of a revolutionary stance in an election was not ruled out. To
enter parliament 'as rebels' meant entering with a
decisive mandate from a conscious electorate to
prevent the state from being used against the will of a
socialist majority. Like the Sinn Fein tactic, which
was used successfully by those whose sole concern
was to be elected in order to delegitimize the power of
the British state in Ireland, the function of socialist
rebel MPs would not be to contribute to the
government of capitalism but to incapacitate such a
process. Backed by a victory at the ballot box this
strategy would possess the advantages of both
asserting that a socialist majority existed and allowing
delegates (rather than representatives) of that majority
to legitimize their victory constitutionally whilst
removing the legitimacy of parliament should it be
used to block the will of the majority. As a strategy
for democratic social transformation, which, as we
have seen, was not ruled out by Morris, there is much

[18] See Mark Shipway, *Anti-Parliamentary Communism: The Movement
For Workers' Councils in Britain, 1917–45* (London, 1988), esp. chap.
1, pp. 3–33.

[19] Letter to J. Bruce Glasier, 1 Dec. 1886 in P. Henderson, *The Letters of
William Morris* (London, 1950), pp. 262–4.

to be said for this policy. But in *The Policy of Abstention* Morris makes no allowance for this strategy. Why?

Two assumptions by Morris determined his preference for a non-parliamentary strategy. Firstly, an inability in his own mind to separate the use of the ballot box from the advocacy of a reform programme. Secondly, a belief that there could be no establishment of socialism without violent force which would surely be used by the conservative minority against the revolutionary majority, and it would be best not to encourage illusions of peaceful transformation in the minds of those who would have to fight for their principles. The revolutionary scenario described in chapter XVII of *News From Nowhere* (although not necessarily to be read as Morris's sole blueprint for revolution) reflects this assumption.

How valid were these two assumptions? More than once in *The Policy of Abstention* – and elsewhere – Morris takes it as given that any party standing for election must offer a programme of reforms which represent a lesser aim than its actual objective. Yet we have already alluded to two examples of election campaigning which did not do that: the SLP in the USA which, after 1900, stood in elections on a single-issue revolutionary platform; and Sinn Feinn which, though a nationalist rather than socialist party, offered voters a single policy and no reforms to be enacted by its candidates if elected. Other examples could be offered. So what would prevent the Socialist League from standing for election with the expressed objective of not reforming capitalism but seeking its abolition? Would not a substantial number of principled votes for such a position suggest more political organization than for socialists to be urged to merely abstain and add their unused ballot papers to countless and uncounted other abstentions?

The argument concerning force would seem to strengthen rather than weaken the case for winning at the polls, for surely little would do more to damage the legitimacy of a minority assault upon the majority's will than its formal defeat in accordance with its own constitutional rules. Less than four months after he first delivered *The Policy of Abstention* Morris saw the vivid brutality of the organized state, commanded by the Home Secretary and his parliamentary colleagues, when the police riot against workers marching in support of the unemployed took place on Bloody Sunday, 13 November 1887. Before then Morris had entertained hopes that the paid forces of the state, being themselves only wage slaves in uniform, would come to the support of a socialist majority in the event of a violent conflict. 'What would happen when they saw the workers were in earnest?' he asked, 'The cannon would be turned round, the butts of muskets would go up, and the swords and bayonets be sheathed, and these men would say "give us work; let us all be honest men like yourselves."'[20] After Bloody Sunday and his witnessing of the authoritarian regimentation of the trained state hirelings Morris felt rather less optimism about the likelihood of the police and army coming over to the workers' side. What does not add up here, even if the inevitability of violent clashes in a revolutionary situation is accepted, is why Morris believed that leaving the state forces under the

---

[20] Morris's speech reported in the Newcastle Chronicle, quoted in Fiona MacCarthy, *William Morris* (London, 1994), p. 561.

legitimate control of a pro-capitalist parliament should be preferable to seeking the election of a pro-socialist parliament which would have the power to deny legitimacy to militant anti-democrats and reflect the majority will in calling off the hounds.

In *The Policy of Abstention* a strategy of dual power is proposed. The most obvious historical parallel here is Russia after February 1917 when the city soviets (councils) contested power with the warmongering state Duma. A more interesting parallel, popularized on the other side of the Atlantic within a decade after Morris's death, was the policy of the Industrial Workers of the World (IWW, or Wobblies) which, at least at its outset, had a policy of advocating industrial unions, established with socialist intentions and as a means of training for the assumption of social power, while also maintaining a political policy of seeking the election of socialists to state power for the purpose of transferring such power to the industrial unions. (The IWW later dropped its political clause, adopting a position closer to the version of syndicalism proposed by Morris.) Even in the months of dual power in Russia all of the revolutionary parties maintained support for the policy of electoral action, as soon as a democratically-elected Constituent Assembly could be established.

For Morris the key to authority (which, unlike the anarchists, he did not oppose) was that it should be democratically organized. His fear of parliamentary authority rested upon a fundamentally democratic concern, rooted in Marx's thinking, for democratic autonomy; 'individual men cannot shuttle off the business of life onto the shoulders of an abstraction called the State, but must deal with it in conscious association with each other'.[21]   Flawed though his rejection of parliamentary action might have been (the case for its strengths is put more than adequately in the pages which follow), Morris's call to abstain from a society of government and governed, and to actively pursue real participatory democracy ruled by 'the social conscience without which there can be no true society', provides a socialist legacy which offers much to the present in its search for alternatives to the authoritarianism of Left and Right which has characterized so much of the recent past.

Stephen Coleman
The Hansard Society, 1996

[21] William Morris, 'Review of "Looking Backward"', *Commonweal*, vol. 5, 22 June 1889, pp. 194–5.

CONTENTS

THE POLICY OF ABSTENTION

William Morris

THE POLICY OF ABSTENTION (1887)

ALL Socialists who can be considered to have any claim to that title agree in putting forward the necessity of transforming the means of production from individual into common property: that is the least that the party can accept as terms of peace with the capitalists; and obviously they are hard terms of peace for the latter, since they mean the destruction of individualist capital. This minimum which we claim therefore is a very big thing: its realization would bring about such a revolution as the world has not yet seen, and all minor reforms of civilization which have been thought of or would be possible to think of would be included in it: no political party has ever had a programme at once so definite and so inclusive: many Socialists would be satisfied if the party were to put forward nothing save this claim; and if there were no party which put forward anything else I think all Socialists would feel themselves bound to support the party that had this platform to the utmost: but the shadow of the stupendous revolution which the abolition of private property in the means of production would bring about is cast upon our present opinions and policy. We cannot help speculating

434

on what would be the consequences of the change, and how it would affect what would be left of our civilization, not only as to the production of wealth, but also as to religion, morals, the relation between the sexes, the methods of government or administration, and in short the whole of social life: of most of these matters I shall say nothing further in this paper, but will only briefly allude to matters directly connected with industrial production, and the administration of affairs.

Now amongst Socialists there are some who think that the abolition of private property in the means of production only would bring about a stable condition of society which would carry out communism no further, that the *product* of labour working on raw material and aided by instruments which were common property, should not be common, but would be the prize of energy, industry, and talent: 'to each one according to his deeds.' In case there are any non-Socialists in the room, I may point out that this condition of things would be quite different from the present one, under which people can live idle and force others to work for them if they chance to be possessed of a share in the monopoly of the means of production, which is the privilege of their class; if it could be carried out and maintained without artificial bolstering up, it would be that real 'career open to talent' which Napoleon ignorantly supposed his bourgeois Caesarism was to sustain: but some of us suppose that without such artificial bolstering up it would lead us back again into a new form of class society; that those who developed the greatest share of certain qualities not necessarily the most useful to the community, would gain a superior position from which they would be able to force the less gifted to serve them. And in fact those who limit the revolution of Socialism to the abolition of private property merely in the means of production do contemplate a society in which production shall be in tutelage to the state; in which the centralized state would draw arbitrarily the line where public property ends and private

435

property begins, would interfere with inheritance and with the accumulation of wealth, and in many ways would act as a master, and take the place of the old masters: acting with benevolent intention indeed, but with conscious artificiality and by means of the employment of obvious force which would be felt everywhere and would sometimes at least be evaded or even resisted, and so at last might even bring on a new revolution which might lead us backward for a while, or might carry us forward into a condition of true Communism according to the ripeness or unripeness of the State Socialist revolution: in short to some of us it seems as if this view of Socialism simply indicates the crystallization of what can only be a transitional condition of society, and cannot in itself be stable: we on the other hand consider the aim of Socialism to be equality of condition: since the production of wares and the service of the community must always be a matter of co-operation; you cannot, if it were desirable, find out what each man's 'deeds' are; and if you could, we see no reason for setting up a higher standard of livelihood for A because he can turn out more work than B, while the needs of the two are just the same: if society is to be of use to B, it must defend him against the tyranny of nature; and if instead of defending him against nature it turns round and helps her to punish poor B for not being born of the same capacity of developing muscle as A, society is a traitor to B, and he if he be a man of any spirit will be rebel against it. We Communists therefore say that it is not possible really to proportion the reward to the labour, and that if you were able to do so you would still have to redress by charity the wrongs of the weak against the strong, you would still not be able to avoid a poor-law: the due exercise of one's energies for the common good and capacity for personal use we say form the only claims to the possession of wealth, and this right of property, the only safeguard against the creation of fresh privilege, which would have to be abolished like the old privilege. All this is admitted by many who will not call

436

themselves Communists, because they do not wish anything to be put before people at present except the transitional state of things: and many of us Communists for our part are willing to admit that the communization of the means of production will inevitably lead to the communization of the products of labour also, and that, as I began by saying, it is a programme sufficiently big to put before the people of our generation, and the consequences of its realization can for the present be left to take care of themselves. So you see there is hardly a question at issue on this point between the Socialists and the Communists. I will therefore assume in this paper that the immediate object of Socialists is the transformation of the raw material and the instruments of labour from private into common property, and then go on to inquire what are the means by which that object can be carried out. I would not have spoken as to the different opinions about the aims of Socialism if I had not felt that those opinions, as I have said elsewhere, would be likely to influence people's views as to the means of its realization. The opinions as to the means are not quite conterminous with the two schools of so-called Socialists and Communists, but they are nearly so, and naturally, since the former are prepared to accept as a necessity a central all-powerful authoritative government, a reformed edition, one may say, of the state government at present existing; whereas the Communists, though they are not clear as to what will take the place of that in the meanwhile, are at least clear that when the habit of social life is established, nothing of the kind of authoritative central government will be needed or endured.

The moderate Socialists or those who can see nothing but the transitional period therefore, believe in what may be called a system of cumulative reforms as the means towards the end; which reforms must be carried out by means of Parliament and a bourgeois executive, the only legal power at present existing, while the Communists believe that it would be waste of time for the Socialists to expend their energy in furthering reforms which so far from bringing us nearer to Socialism would rather serve to bolster up the present state of things; and not believing in the efficacy of reforms, they can see no reason for attempting to use Parliament in any way; except perhaps by holding it up as an example to show what a contemptible thing a body can be which poses as the representative of a whole nation, and which really represents nothing but the firm determination of the privileged or monopolist class to stick to their privilege and monopoly till they are *forced* to relinquish it.

Well there are, it seems, two policies before us, which, if you will allow me, I will call for short the Policy of Parliamentary Action, and the Policy of Abstention. But before I go further I must say that though the question as to which of the two policies is to be adopted in the long run is doubtless a most interesting one, yet that at present there is only one policy open to us, that of preaching Socialism to as many people as we can get at. This no doubt seems to many a dull job, offering no rewards to any of us in the way of notoriety or position: but after all it is the way which all new creeds have to go on, and if we neglect it in our haste or impatience, we shall never come to the point at which more definite action will be forced upon us.

Now as to these two policies I will not dwell on the first, not because I do not agree with it, as I do not, but because it has been put before you often enough and with copious enough arguments and advocacy: to convince the voters that they ought to send Socialists to Parliament who should try to get measures passed in the interests of the working-classes, and gradually transform the present Parliament, which is a mere instrument in the hands of the monopolizers of the means of production, into a body which should destroy monopoly, and then direct and administer the freed labour of the community. That is I think a correct statement of the views of those who further the policy of parliamentary action.

Such a scheme or plan of campaign will sound practical and reasonable to many, or to most if you will: and al- though it is right, in considering any scheme, to consider the drawbacks to it, yet even when we admit that those drawbacks exist, we do not necessarily condemn the scheme: so I will not at present say anything about the drawbacks which after all must be patent to those even who think the policy a good and necessary one. Indeed if no other plan of campaign were possible for the attack on monopoly, we should have to accept all drawbacks, stifle all doubts and carry it out with all our might. But there is another plan of campaign possible which I must lay before you at rather greater length under the nick-name, as I said, of the Policy of Abstention.

This plan is founded on the necessity of making the class-struggle clear to the workers, of pointing out to them that while monopoly exists they can only exist as its slaves: so that the Parliament and all other institutions at present existing are maintained for the purpose of upholding this slavery; that their wages are but slaves' rations, and if they were increased tenfold would be nothing more: that while the bourgeois rule lasts they can indeed take part in it, but only on the terms that they shall do nothing to attack the grand edifice of which their slavery is the foundation. Nay more than that: that they are asked to vote and send repre- sentatives to Parliament (if 'working-men' so much the better) that they may point out what concessions may be necessary for the ruling class to make in order that the slavery of the workers may last on: in a word that to vote for the continuance of their own slavery is all the parliamentary action that they will be allowed to take under the present regime: Liberal Associations, Radical clubs, working men members are at present, and Socialist members will be in the future, looked on with complacency by the governing classes as serving towards the end of propping the stability of robber society in the safest and least troublesome man- ner by beguiling them to take part in their own government. A great invention, and well worthy of the reputation of the Briton for practicality—and swindling! How much better than the coarse old-world iron repression of that blunderer Bismark, which at once irritates and consolidates the working-men, and depends for its temporary success even on the absence of such accidents as a sudden commercial crisis or a defeat of the German army.

The Policy of Abstention then is founded on this view: that the interests of the two classes, the workers and the capitalists, are irreconcilable, and as long as the capitalists exist as a class, they having the monopoly of the means of production, have all the power of ordered and legal society; but on the other hand that the use of this power to keep down a wronged population, which feels itself wronged, and is organizing itself for illegal resistance when the opportunity shall serve, would impose such a burden on the governing classes as they will not be able to bear; and they must finally break down under it, and take one of two courses, either of them the birth of fear acting on the instinct to prolong and sustain their life which is essential in all organisms. One course would be to try the effect of wholesale concessions, or what seemed to be such in order to diminish the number of the discontented; and this course would be almost certain to have a partial success; but I feel sure not so great a success in delaying revolution, as it would have if taken with the expressed agreement of Socialist representatives in Parliament: in the latter case the concessions would be looked upon as a victory; whereas if they were the work of a hated government from which the people were standing aloof, they would be dreaded as a bait, and scorned as the last resource of a tyranny growing helpless. The other course which a government recognized as a mere tyranny would be driven to by a policy of abstention, would be stern repression of whatever seemed to be dangerous to it; that is to say of the opinions and aspirations of the working classes as a whole: for in England at least there would be no attempt to adopt this course until opinion was so grown and so organized that the danger to monopoly seemed imminent. In short the two courses are fraud and force, and doubtless in a commercial country like this the resources of fraud would be exhausted before the ruling class betook itself to open force.

Now I say that either of these courses will indicate a breakdown of the class government, and in my belief it would be driven to them more speedily by abstaining from rendering it any help in the form of pushing palliative measures in parliament, and thereby pointing out to it a way to stave off revolution; but it is a matter of course that this abstention which we put forward as a weapon to drive the ruling class to extremities must be backed up by widespread opinion, by the conviction in a vast number of persons that the basis of society must be changed, and labour set free by the abolition of monopoly in the means of production, which monopoly is at present the basis of our society. But of course the necessity for obtaining this body of opinion is not confined to those Socialists that advocate abstention from parliamentary action: the making of Socialists must be a preliminary to the settling of the question, What are Socialists to do? Now it is clear that the first step towards this end is the putting forward of the principles of Socialism, preaching them as widely as possible; this is practically all that up to the present we have been able to do, and whatever success we have had in the undertaking (people will have different opinions about that) we have worked at it with very considerable energy. But it has been said that the mere preaching of principles, however much the acceptance of them may involve definite action in the future, is not enough; that you must offer your recruits something to do beyond merely swelling the army of preachers in one way or another. Well I agree with that, so far as this, that the time comes in such a movement as ours when it is ready to change from a mere intellectual movement into a movement of action, and that that time must be taken advantage of, and if there is no good plan of action ready the movement

441

will certainly take up a bad one in default of none at all. The plan offered by some of our friends I have stated before as an attempt to get hold of Parliament by constitutional means in order to use it for unconstitutional purposes: that plan I think a bad one for reasons that I have hinted at already and shall try to state more fully and consecutively before I have done. Yet if the plan has its birth from anything more solid than impatience, and the weariness that is sure to beset a small minority preaching revolution, it is a hopeful sign that it should be put forward, and its being put forward in a manner compels us who do not agree with it to put forward some alternative to it, even though we think, as I confess I for one do, that all plans of action are at present premature.

Well, I have put forward one part of our plan, viz. a strict holding aloof from taking part in a government whose object is the maintenance of monopoly: you will say of course that is not action: but I say that it is, if combined as it is sure to be, with the resolute preaching of principles with a view to action when that becomes possible without sullying it by alliance with the very tyranny which we are leagued to destroy: it then becomes the foundation of that great instrument of attack on a majority of brute force known as 'the boycott.' For before we can begin to use that we must be bound together by the full consciousness that we are oppressed by a class who cannot help oppressing us and whose oppression we cannot help resisting.

But again you may say before we can begin boycotting we must have numbers; how are they to be obtained otherwise than by interesting a large body of people in reforms which will have a plausible look of bettering their position? That is a shrewd question, but I hope I can answer it satisfactorily. It will be our business to give a new turn to all the smouldering discontent of the workers and the perpetual struggle of labour against capital which is now feebly and incompletely organized by the Trades Unions. Those bodies, which grew into power at a time when the principle

442

of capitalism was not attacked, can until they are radically
altered only deal with its accidental abuses; and they have
also the essential quality of being benefit societies, which
would be all very well if they denied the rights of capital
altogether and were complete fighting bodies; because the
benefit society business would then mean just the army
chest; but at present when the rights of capital are admitted
and all that is claimed is a proportional share in the profits,
it means a kind of relief to the employers, an additional
poor-rate levied from the workers. As things now go the
position of the Trades Unions, as anything but benefit
societies, has become an impossible one; the long and short
of what they say to the masters is this: We are not going to
interfere with your management of our affairs except so far
as we can reduce your salary as our managers. We acknowledge that we are machines and that you are the hands that
guide us; but we will pay as little as we can help for your
guidance and fight you on that point. Well the masters can
and do reply: My friends, you are making an end not of
our profits only but of our function of guidance, and since
you are, as you admit, our machines, when our guidance is
gone, gone also is your livelihood. No, we know your interests better than you do yourselves, and shall resist your
feeble attempts to reduce our salaries; and since we organ-
ize your labour and the market of the world which it supplies, we shall manage your wages amongst other matters.

Now that's the blind alley which the Trades Unions have
now got into: I say again if they are determined to have masters to manage their affairs, they must expect in turn to pay
for that luxury. To go any further they must get out of that
blind alley and into the open highway that leads to Socialism. They must aim at managing their own business, which
is indeed the business of the world: remembering that the
price they pay for their so-called captains of industry is no
mere money-payment—no mere tribute which once paid
leaves them free to do as they please, but an authoritative
ordering of the whole tenor of their lives, what they shall

443

eat, drink, wear, what houses they shall have, books, or newspapers rather, they shall read, down to the very days on which they shall take their holidays like a drove of cattle driven out from the stable to grass.

Well, I say that the real business of us propagandists is to instil this aim of the workers becoming the masters of their own destinies, their own lives, and this can be effected when a sufficient number of them are convinced of the fact by the establishment of a vast labour organization—the federation according to their crafts, if you will, of all the workmen who have awoke to the fact that they are the slaves of monopoly, and therefore being awaked, its rebels also; men who are convinced that the raw material and instruments of labour can only belong to those who can use them: let them announce that transformation of these things into common property as their programme, and look upon anything else they may have to do before they have conquered that programme, as so much necessary work by the way to enable them to live till they have marched to the great battlefield. Let them settle e.g. what wages are to be paid by their temporary managers, what number of hours it may be expedient to work; let them arrange for the filling of their military chest, the care of the sick, the unemployed, the dismissed: let them learn also how to administer their own affairs. Time and also power fails me to give any scheme for how all this could be done; but granting the formation of such a body I cannot help thinking that for the two last purposes they might make use of the so-called plan of co-operation.

Well now, as to this great labour body I expect all Socialists to agree with me in advocating its formation, and also to admit that the furtherance of such a body is very great work and worth all our efforts to bring about; where some Socialists will differ from me will be that they will not be able to see why all this should not go on pari passu with Parliamentary action.

Well, I also expect them to agree with me in thinking it

necessary in pointing out to the workers the irreconcil-
ability between true free labour and individualist capitalism; surely in order to drive this fact home, it is necessary to
keep the two camps of labour and monopoly as distinct as
possible.

If such a labour organization as I have been putting before you were set on foot, and it took root and grew, and
spread as it would if things were ripe either for that or
another form of preparation for action, what would be the
condition of things in the country? On the one hand the
useful classes banded together for the purpose of a change
in the basis of society which would acknowledge their
usefulness and the usefulness of all others; which would
abolish classes altogether; on the other hand a committee
of the useless or monopolist class, authoritative because it
holds the sway over the army, navy and police, but with no
power of doing anything but launching that power of destruction at those who make all that is made, and so des-
troying their own livelihood along with that of their enemy;
with no power of bribing them by concessions, because the
popular party claim one thing only, the abolition of the
class that on its side claims to rule. What could come out of
the opposition of these two forces, the useful working society, and the useless class that claims nothing but to live on
the former? What could come of this opposition but destruction of the useless? Could armed reaction triumph?
Certainly only for a while; that at the worst; but probably it
would not even appear to conquer: there would be perhaps
some feeble attempt at putting down the popular combination by force; but it would be half-hearted and would soon
come to an end if that party were true to itself and felt its
power in combination. What would be the use of the
authoritative government making laws for people who
denied its right, and felt it to be their duty to evade or resist
them at every point? Nothing would come of them, they
would simply drop dead. And now mark that this movement, this force for the revolution that we all call for can

445

only be fully evolved from this conscious opposition of the two powers, monopolist authority and free labour: everything that tends to mask that opposition, to confuse it, weakens the popular force, and gives a new lease of life to the reaction, which can indeed create nothing, can only hang on a while by favour of such drags on such weaknesses of the popular force. If our own people are forming part of parliament, the instruments of the enemy, they are helping to make the very laws we will not obey. Where is the enemy then? What are we to do to attack him? The enemy is a principle, you say: true, but the principle must be embodied; and how can it be better embodied than in that assembly delegated by the owners of monopoly to defend monopoly at all points? to smooth away the difficulties of the monopolists even at the expense of apparent sacrifice of their interests 'to the amelioration of the lot of the working classes'? to profess friendship with the so-called moderates (as if there could be any moderation in dealing with a monopoly, anything but for or against)? in short to detach a portion of the people from the people's side, to have it in their midst helpless, dazed, wearied with ceaseless compromise, or certain defeat, and yet to put it before the world as the advanced guard of the revolutionary party, the representative of all that is active or practical of the popular party?

This is the advantage not speculative but certain which sending Socialist members to Parliament would hand over to the reactionists: let us try rather, I say once more, to sustain a great body of workers outside Parliament, call it the labour parliament if you will, and when that is done be sure that its decrees will be obeyed and not those of the Westminster Committee. And whatever may be said of the possibility of such a plan in other countries, in Britain it is possible, because the mere political position of the workers is better here than elsewhere in Europe; even though there are countries in which the suffrage is more extended: the habit of democracy has gained sway over those persons and parties even who in feeling and aspiration are least democratic; and they cannot do what they would, so that any English government Tory as well as Liberal is ham- pered in its reactionary attempts and does not dare to attack the expression of opinion openly unless driven to despair; the Labour Combination I have been putting before you will not be openly attacked by its enemy the Parliament till it is too late, till it has done the first part of its work by instilling hope in the whole of the workers, the hope of their managing their own affairs and freeing themselves from Monopoly.

Now it will be said and of course truly that the advocates of parliamentary action amongst us are just as desirous of seeing this great labour organization established as we are: but in the first place I cannot help thinking that the scheme of parliament would be found in practice to stand in the way of the formation of that widespread organization with its singleness of aim and directness of action which it seems to me is what we want: that the effort towards success in parliament will swallow up all other effort, that such success in short will come to be looked upon as the end. However, you may say that this mistake can be guarded against and avoided; I am far from sure that it can be, but let that pass: the organization I am thinking of would have a serious point of difference from any that could be formed as a part of a parliamentary plan of action: its aim would be to act directly, whatever was done in it would be done by the people themselves; there would consequently be·no possibility of compromise, of the association becoming anything else than it was intended to be; nothing could take its place: before all its members would be put but one alternative to complete success, complete failure, namely. Can as much be said for any plan involving the representatives of the people forming a part of a body whose purpose is the continuous enslavement of the people?

I think I can explain better what is in my mind as to these two plans of action if I give a sketch of what I think

447

would happen if either were adopted: only understand I don't mean to prophesy, only to try to draw out the logical consequences of that adoption. Take the policy of abstention first, and start from where we are now, the Socialist movement still in its intellectual stage: a stage at which only those who have thought about the matter see the necessity of placing society on a new basis; a time in which the necessity is not forced upon them by their immediate needs. While this lasts only those will join the movement with sincerity who have intelligence enough to accept principles and to forecast events from them; but they will form a solid body impossible to suppress or to be discouraged by hope deferred just for that reason; they will teach others, and be taught by the teaching; and as the approaching break-down of the monopolist system comes closer conviction will be forced on the minds of more and more people, till at last the mere necessities of life will force the main part of the workers to join them; and they will find in them no mere aggregation of discontent, but a body of persons who can teach the aims of Socialism and consult coolly about its methods. They will then be grown into that powerful body I have spoken of, the representative of the society of production, the direct opposition to the society of exploitation which will be represented by the constitutional government, the laws it has made and supports and the organized brute force which it wields. The revolutionary body will find its duties divided into two parts, the maintenance of its people while things are advancing to the final struggle, and resistance to the constitutional authority, including the evasion or disregard of the arbitrary laws of the latter. Its chief weapons during this period will be co-operation and boycotting, the latter including all strikes that may be necessary: whether it will be driven to use further weapons depends on the attitude of the Reaction: that party will probably be paralysed before the steady advance of revolution, and will, as in France in the earlier revolution, use its mechanical brute-force in a wavering undecided half-hearted manner: it is by no means certain now, as it was The Policy in the Chartist times, that the threat of the imminence of a general strike would be the signal for the reaction to launch Abstention its army upon the people. Indeed supposing such a crisis at hand, the revolutionists might forestall the actual battle by using for once and for a definite purpose its enemy par- liament by sending members to outvote the reactionists on that occasion: by doing which if they did not get actual command of the army &c. they would at least paralyse its action by making that action of doubtful legality: for though a revolutionist may fight well with a rope round his neck, such a necklace is an awkward adornment for your counter-revolutionist. I have nothing further to say of the revolutionists beyond this stage except that the long ex- perience they would have had in their earlier stage of a labour organization, of administering the affairs of the real producers, and still more the experience of administration they would have spread during that period would make the Morrow of the Revolution a much easier time to them than it would be to a party that had not already learned to help itself. For the rest I should say that our friend Paul Lafar- gue's late article in *Commonweal* points out clearly enough the direction of the steps to be taken in the re-organization of society.

Now for a brief history of the plan of parliamentary ac- tion: Starting from the same point as the abstentionists they have to preach an electioneering campaign as an abso- lute necessity, and to set about it as soon as possible: they will then have to put forward a programme of reforms de- duced from the principles of Socialism, which we will admit they will always keep to the front as much as possible; they will necessarily have to appeal for support (i.e. votes) to a great number of people who are not convinced Socialists, and their programme of reforms will be the bait to catch these votes: and to the ordinary voter it will be this bait which will be the matter of interest, and not the principle for whose furtherance they will be intended to act as an instrument: when the voting recruit reads the manifesto of a parliamentary body, he will scarcely notice the statement of principles which heads it, but he will eagerly criticize the proposals of measures to be carried which he finds below it: and yet if he is to be honestly dealt with, he will have to be told that these measures are not put forward as a solution of the social question, but are—in short, ground-bait for him so that he may be led at last to search into and accept the real principles of Socialism. So that it will be impossible to deal with him honestly, and the Socialist members when they get into Parliament will represent a heterogeneous body of opinion, ultra-radical, democratic, discontented non-politicals, rather than a body of Social-ists; and it will be their opinions and prejudices that will sway the action of the members in Parliament. With these fetters on them the Socialist members will have to act, and whatever they propose will have to be a mere matter of compromise: yet even those measures they will not carry: because long before their party gets powerful enough to form even a formidable group for alliance with other par-ties, one section or other of ordinary politicians will dish them, and will carry measures that will pass current for being the very thing the Socialists have been asking for; because once get Socialist M.P.s, and to the ordinary public they will be the representatives of the only Socialists. Now the result of such a 'success' will be the necessity of a new Socialist programme on the one hand and on the other an accession of strength to the moderates; and this kind of thing will go on again and again with at least an appearance of defeat every time; and every time a temporary gain not for the Socialists but either for the reactionists or at least for the progressive Democratic party. Which latter (always a weak and inefficient party in this country) will be to a cer-tain extent permeated with a kind of semi-Socialism, but will by that very fact lose many of their members to the 'mode-rate' reactionists on one hand, though on the other they will offer a recruiting ground for the Socialists. Well so it will

450

go on till either the Socialist party in Parliament disappears
into the advanced Democratic party, or until they look
round and find that they, still Socialists, have done nothing
but give various opportunities to the reactionists for widen-
ing the basis of monopoly by creating a fresh middle-class
under the present one, and so staving off the day of the
great change. And when they become conscious of that and
parliamentary action has been discovered to be a failure,
what can they do but begin all over again, and try to form
the two camps, each of them conscious of their true position
of being the one monopolists, and the other the slaves of
monopoly.

Yet even supposing that they succeed and by means of
tormenting the constitutional Parliament into cumulative
reforms manage to bring us to the crisis of revolution, their
difficulties would be far from an end then: for they would
then would have to govern a people who had rather been
ignorantly betrayed into Socialism than have learned to
accept it as an understood necessity: and in governing such
a people they would have this disadvantage, that they
would not have the education which their helping in the
organization of the society of production would have given
them, teaching them as it were by the future and forming
the habits of social life without which any scheme of
Socialism is but the mill-wheel without the motive power.
Their very success would lead to counter revolution; because they would have to repress the ignorance which they
had not grappled with in their militant times, by brute
force. Doubtless this counter revolution would lead us in
the long run into a condition of true society again: but need
we go through all that trouble, confusion and misery? let us
begin to work against the counter revolution, by being sure
that we who call ourselves Socialists understand what we are
aiming at, and should feel at home in our new country when
we got there—we and all that we lead into the new country.

But I will say no more at present against that parliamentary action, which some of our friends think the step now

451

necessary to the furtherance of Socialism, but will rather try
to sum up what I have had to say in favour of the plan of
abstention from that action. It is above all things necessary
that the working-classes should feel their present position,
that they understand that they are in an inferior position
not accidentally but as a necessary consequence of the position of the classes that live by monopoly. When they have
learnt this lesson they will learn with it the necessity for a
change in the basis of society: they are strong enough if
they combine duly to bring that change about; but their
due combination depends on their knowing that from the
present rulers of society they will get nothing but concessions intended to perpetuate their present slavery: they
must know they are invited to vote and take some part in
government in order that they may help their rulers to find
out what must be conceded, and what may be refused to the
workers; and to give an appearance of freedom of action to
them. But the workers can form an organization which
without heeding Parliament can force from the rulers what
concessions may be necessary in the present and whose aim
would be the total abolition of the monopolist classes and
rule. The action such an organization would be compelled
to take would educate its members in administration, so
that on the morrow of the revolution they would be able,
from a thorough knowledge of the wants and capabilities of
the workers, to carry on affairs with the least possible
amount of blunders, and would do almost nothing that
would have to be undone, and thereby offer no opportunity
to the counter revolution. This seems to me the direct way
to the realization of Socialism, and therefore in the long run
the shortest way. I admit that it will ask for qualities of
patience, devotion and forgetfulness of self in its pioneers,
but it is a commonplace to say that impatience, carelessness
and egotism are hindrances to any cause, and have to be
fought against; and if Socialism militant cannot reckon on
enlisting persons who are somewhat above the average,
and on staving off others who are a good deal below it,

452

there is nothing to be done but to sit still and see what will The Policy
happen. That however we shall not and cannot do; some- of
thing we must do however fatalistic we may be: my hope Abstention
is that what we shall do will show us to be Socialists in
essence and in spirit even now when we cannot be Socialists
economically.

SOCIALISM

AND

RADICALISM

A LECTURE READ BEFORE THE HAMMERSMITH SOCIALIST SOCIETY

BY

JOHN CARRUTHERS

Price One Penny

PUBLISHED BY
THE HAMMERSMITH SOCIALIST SOCIETY
KELMSCOTT HOUSE, UPPER MALL, HAMMERSMITH
LONDON, W.
1894

SOCIALISM AND RADICALISM

A FEW years ago, when the band of those who openly called themselves Socialists was small, there was little difference of opinion among them as to whether they should take part in the ordinary conflict for power among the Radicals, the Whigs, and the Tories. They were all agreed that, although the Radical programme contained many things, such as extension of the suffrage, free education, &c., which were in themselves worth having, it was not their business to agitate for it. The Radicals, it was argued, would attend to Radical matters, which are, after all, of little importance, since the whole programme would, if obtained, have no practical influence in improving the lives of the working classes. Were Socialists to join in the agitation for obtaining these slight concessions it was felt that they would be apt to forget how relatively unimportant these are, and that their Socialism, being set aside for the sake of lesser things, might degenerate into a mere theoretical belief.

Within the last few years, however, a great change has come over the country in its expressed political opinions. A dozen years ago a Socialist meeting could scarcely muster as active members more than the sacred twelve; but they were all real and earnest Socialists, having no sort of doubt that the doctrines they met to discuss and to teach to each other would, sooner or later, be accepted by everyone all over the world. They were equally convinced that Socialism is not a mere theoretical faith, but is a practical system of industrial organisation, which could be made at once the actual working system, were it the wish of the working classes that this should be done. The true work of Socialists was felt to be that of preaching the new doctrine by word and by pen, and of endeavouring to arouse the working classes from the torpid conservatism which alone keeps them in their present state of economic slavery. That the upper and middle classes should also be converted was, of course, also desired, but Socialists troubled themselves less about this since they knew that freedom can come only from the determination of the unfree to break their bonds, and that the conversion of the rich was therefore unimportant, while it would also be as difficult to effect as to make a camel go through the eye of a needle.

Now, however, "we are all Socialists," in name at least; in every town in the kingdom Socialist Societies are to be found; the trades unions have collectively adopted the fundamental article of the faith, namely, that all implements of production ought to be the collective property of the people, and not of any individual; and, above all, a Labour Party has been formed, the professed object of whose leaders is to drive into the same camp all, whether they call themselves Radical or Whig or Tory, who do not take the wellbeing of the working class as the sole aim of their legislation.

This great change has introduced among Socialists a good deal of difference of opinion as to their proper political action, some inclining to join the Labour Party, while others hesitate to do so. Had the progress made by Socialism been as deep as it is wide, no doubt the time for political action would have come, but this is far from being the case. Of the hundreds of thousands, or even millions, who would now subscribe to the Socialist doctrine that land and all other implements of production ought to cease to be private property, comparatively few intend to try to abolish at once and for ever the whole capitalist system, or even wish that it shall be at once abolished. Their conversion to Socialism is not much more real than was the conversion to Christianity of most of the early converts. Whole tribes and nations used to come to the preachers to be baptised, but when they got back to their homes they used to continue as before to worship their old gods, perhaps under new names—Jupiter, perhaps, got christened Jehovah, and Vesta, Mary—but the worship was exactly the same as before, and although the people called themselves Christians they really remained heathen.

We see exactly the same thing taking place with very many of the nominal converts to Socialism. The trades unions, for instance, received public baptism at their Belfast meeting by passing the Socialist resolution, that the implements of production ought to be nationalised. This, however, meant no more than such a vague general approval of Socialism as the early converts gave to Christianity. It did not mean that trades unionists were going to stop agitating for their old objects and to take up an entirely new programme, but it only meant that they would continue to worship Radicalism under the new name of Socialism. When, for instance, the Lords practically threw out the Employers' Liability Bill, the workmen assembled in Hyde Park to protest angrily against their action, although they took no steps whatever to emphasise the belief they had just publicly professed, that the well-being of the working classes can be obtained only by abolishing employers altogether instead of by merely lessening their privileges.

Had the men been true converts they would have known that the Employers' Liability Bill was a mere trifle, useful, perhaps, as far as it went, but which would have no practical influence in bettering the condition of the working classes. Let us grant that a far better bill were passed than the wretched thing that was amended, as they call it, by the Lords, and that every man who got his legs or arms shattered would be maintained in what a modern workman would call comfort for the rest of his life, and that the widows and children of those who were killed would be defended against hunger and cold. This is much more than the bill of last session would have granted, but what practical effect would it have on the poverty of England? Are there no poor besides those who have been maimed in their work, or whose bread-winners have been killed by accidents arising from the fault of the employer? Such a question is, of course, absurd. Even though all these people were provided for, it would be like taking a bucketful of water out of the Thames by way of lessening a flood, and the mass of poverty left would not be perceptibly lessened.

Still it will be said, Is not half a loaf better than no bread? and although the bill would not do much good it would do some. Must not, therefore, Socialists, and others who want to improve the condition of the workmen, become Radicals, in so far as to agitate for the bill and try to get it passed? This is the question on which Socialists are now a good deal divided in opinion, and on which I hope our discussion this evening will turn.

Were it really a choice between half a loaf and no bread there can be little doubt that we ought to take the half loaf, and to agitate in order that we might get it, thus becoming good Radicals and good workers at every election. It is not, however, a question of half a loaf or no bread, for it is just as easy to get the whole of the loaf as the half of it, if only we could make up our minds that we really wanted the whole. One would think from the way this subject is often discussed that our good friends the employers of labour are burning with a desire to give the workmen, from sheer brotherly love and good fellowship, certain advantages, and are prevented from carrying out their kindly intention by the Lords. This, however, is not the case. It is an essential part of the whole system of capitalism that the employers shall give to the workmen no more than they are obliged to give. The whole relation between masters and men is one of war, and the masters will give all that the war compels them to give, but no more. Here in England the men have the power of getting, peaceably and legally, whatever they choose to ask for, and the only reason they don't get the whole loaf is that they only ask for the half, and are not even agreed in asking for that.

The extreme Radical programme is the half loaf which some of the workmen have, with half earnestness, asked for, but the majority of them have taken very little interest in the matter, mainly, perhaps, because they think the half loaf would do them little good, and that it is not bread at all but only a stone. Nor would they be far wrong in so thinking, for under the present system, however it may be patched and mended, there is no hope of economic well-being for the working classes.

We have in New Zealand a clear example to show us how little the most extreme Radicalism can do. There is a country with a glorious climate, a fertile soil, abundance of coal, iron, gold, and other minerals, fine harbours all round the coasts, and which is so far from being over populated that, although it is larger than England, it has a population not much larger than that of Manchester. Surely, with all these natural advantages, intelligent and industrious workmen ought to be able to live in comfort and security, and yet we know that poverty and want of employment are as common there as in England. The forefathers of these men, who knew nothing of the steam engine, and who, owing to the scarcity and dearness of iron, were obliged to till their land with clumsy wooden spades and ploughs and to weave their clothing with looms at which a New Zealander would laugh, not only lived in security that their daily bread would be daily earned, but could also spare from the production of necessaries enough labour to cover the land with noble and costly buildings, and this New Zealand assuredly cannot afford to do. What natural advantage had the England of six hundred years ago over the New Zealand of to-day that more than made up for the ignorance of Englishmen of mechanical science, and the consequent inefficiency of their labour? As far as we can see, England had no natural superiority, but on the other hand was inferior at every point—it had, at all events, a worse climate and worse land. It had one, and only one, advantage; the capitalist system of government was still in an undeveloped form, and this is a far greater advantage to the working classes than any efficiency of labour that science can give. Even New Zealand has, in its short life, enjoyed this advantage, and while the capitalists there were not yet settled down into correct commercial methods of working, the labouring class enjoyed abundance and were never out of work. No sooner, however, did the country begin to get settled, and banks and money exchanges to get established, than meetings of the unemployed and all the other such concomitants of capitalist production began to appear, and are now become part of the daily life of the colony. The same rapid change from comfort to poverty has befallen the working classes of Canada, Victoria, New South Wales, and all the other "flourishing" colonies, while the United States, as becomes its greater area and the proverbial shrewdness and energy of its capitalists, exemplifies the same law on a scale of colossal magnitude.

Yet all these countries enjoy all and more than all that even the most extreme Radicals propose to get for England and which when gotten will, they tell us, raise the working classes to comfort. They have no royal family to maintain, no House of Lords to mend or end, no Established Church to disestablish, no army and navy to pay for. They have, in New Zealand at least, universal suffrage, even the women having a vote ; they have "local option" as to the drink traffic, employers' liability bills and eight hours' bills have been passed, members of Parliament are paid, the railways have been nationalised, and most of the waterworks, gasworks, and tramways municipalised. Yet in spite of all this extreme Radicalism, the position of the workmen is getting worse day by day, and it is scarcely to be wondered at that English workmen do not take much interest in legislation which at best can only raise them to the position held by their brothers in New Zealand or New

York, and which is no better than that they hold themselves.

Ought we Socialists to pretend that we believe in these
Radical measures? Ought we to try to induce the working
classes to take an interest in legislation directed to Radical
reform? We know that it would not improve their position
to any practical extent, and that our present political
machinery, although not perfect, nor even as good, from a
Radical point of view, as that of New Zealand, is yet good
enough for all the uses to which a Socialist wants to put it.
We have not universal suffrage, it is true, and the ruling
powers, Liberal and Tory alike, attach such conditions to
the exercise of the franchise as keeps half those from
voting who nominally have the right to do so, but still the
workmen have complete power over the elections if they
would only exercise it, and could, if they liked, make the
Parliament one containing none but working men. This
agitation for Radical reform instead of for Socialist reform
is as sonseless as if we refused to cut our butter until we
had made the butter-knife as sharp as a razor. In England
the knife is already sharp enough, and all energy spent in
further sharpening it is mere waste of time and labour.
In Russia the knife is not sharp enough, and there a
Socialist who wishes to bring about Socialism by peaceful
means may rationally give the labour of his life to the
improvement of the political machine. This was also the
case in England a few years ago, but that day is now gone
by; our machine is now good enough to be set to work, and
labour given to making it better will merely delay the
attainment of the product, for the sake alone of which it
was worth while improving the machine—that is, the
liberation of the workmen from the thraldom of capitalism
and the liberation, at the same time, of the capitalists from
the thraldom of their capital; for capitalism is twice cursed,
it curses him who labours, and him who lives by the product of that labour, while the concerted and organised
labour of freemen would be a joy and a blessing to all.

No real Socialist, knowing, as he must, what trifling
Radicalism is, ought, it appears to me, to mix himself up
in Radical politics. This, however, is done under the plea
that the working classes are not sufficienty advanced to
accept a Socialist programme, Radicalism being all they
are yet prepared for, and that, in order to lead them to
better things, it is necessary to pretend to take a keen

interest in whatever interests them, and thus to graft
Socialism on a Radical stock. I will not discuss the
honesty of such a line of propaganda, but only its practical
wisdom. Many of the early preachers of Christianity
adopted the same policy, but the result was not that the
heathen were converted to true Christianity, but that
Christianity itself became, in all but name, heathenism.
There are many men to-day in Southern India who call
themselves Christians, and who emphasise their Christianity by carrying about in procession a black Jesus and a
black Mary. As, however, the ceremonies with which
they do so are precisely the same as those with which their
heathen fellow-countrymen lead Ramasamy and Jugger-
natu about, the difference in religion is merely one of
names. Do Socialists not run a risk of becoming in the
same way really Radicals when they begin to assimilate
their Socialism to Radicalism, or, rather, has this not
already taken place? Are there not many who once were
Socialists and who still call themselves Socialists, but who
have really become Radicals, and not even of the most
advanced type? Whatever remains of their Socialism has
become a mere pious opinion that it would be an excellent
system of industrial organisation in the planet Saturn, and
that perhaps at some indefinitely far-off time it might be
even introduced into England, but that for the present
only Radical measures deserve the attention of serious
men. It is inevitable that everyone who begins to negoti-
ate with the enemy shall become a traitor, and it is
inevitable that every Socialist who begins to agitate for
Radicalism shall become a Radical. Therefore, I hold,
it is better for us who are Socialists to continue to preach
our doctrines, but not to take part in political quarrels
unless we can do so independently of existing parties who,
however much they may differ in other matters, are agreed
in deadly hatred of Socialism. I don't mean to say that
those who want to vote should not do so, but only that
Socialists should not take an active and leading part in
politics. A man who knows that universal suffrage, for
instance, will do as little good in England as it does in
America may still vote for a man who wants to introduce
it rather than for one who is opposed to it. Its effect, as
far as it goes, is beneficial, although that effect is very
small. He could not, however, make impassioned speeches
in its favour or actively canvass for votes for the candidate

who wanted it without becoming a convert to his own arguments, and becoming a Radical rather than a Socialist.

The Independent Labour Party seems at first sight one which all Socialists ought at once to join, not only as silent voters, but also as active canvassers and propagandists. When we look at the subject, however, a little closer, our duty does not seem so clear. The profession of faith of the party is distinctly Socialist; but is the Socialism real or only nominal? Does the party propose to concern itself with the old class of subjects, or is it animated by a clear and unhesitating conviction that Socialism is the only thing in which the working classes have any real interest, that Socialism is a feasible system of labour organisation that could be introduced at once, and that palliative measures, as they are called, of every kind, are mere trivialities doing no practical good even when they do no harm, as they nearly always do? In the one case certainly we should join the party as active members, but in the other we should give only a silent vote, and should keep our energies for the conversion of the party to real Socialism. Here also we may learn from the experience of those good Radicals, our New Zealand brethren. They have a Labour party, not in a nascent form as with us, but fully developed, with an overwhelming majority in Parliament. Unfortunately their Labour party, although like our own, professing a Socialist creed, is really Radical, working in its endeavours to raise the condition of the labourers only on Radical lines, and, therefore failing to do any good. Its trump card is, as is the case with our own half-hearted Socialists, to find " work for the unemployed." With this end in view, the Government, that is the Labour party, sets aside a large sum of money to be spent in building railways by those who cannot find other work. The result is that when, owing to those ups and downs of trade inseparable from fully organised capitalist production, tailors and shoemakers, spinners and weavers, clerks and engine-drivers, masons and carpenters are thrown out of work they have a pick and shovel put into their hands, and are set to dig for their living. The result of so brilliant a scheme may be easily imagined. To the men, unaccustomed as they are to the use of the pick, the work is heart-breaking slavery, while the wages of the professional navvy are reduced by their competition.

If this be the kind of legislation the Labour party

proposes to introduce, I confess I can't get up much enthusiasm about it. To me it seems absurd that a tailor should be set to digging while there is a needle and a thimble to be got, as he would do better work with the needle than with the pick. He of course also needs cloth, and how is this to be obtained? Simply by keeping the spinners and weavers who are also out of work fully employed, and so throughout the whole society. But, it will be said, that if more weavers and tailors are kept at work by the Government, more clothing will be produced than can be sold at a profit, and the capitalists will have to lessen their production, so that as many men will be thrown out of work on the one hand as will be supplied with work by the Government on the other. This is all quite true; but it only shows the impossibility of doing any good to the working classes on Radical lines or by palliative measures. That is like putting a new piece of cloth into an old garment, and the rent if not made worse will at all events not be made better. Every palliative measure brings its own evil with it, and the evil is generally greater than that it was intended to cure. Unless we make up our minds to have a new garment altogether, we must be prepared to go in rags, for patching will not improve the old one. The New Zealand Labour party have trusted to patching and have done no good, nor will our Labour party be more successful if it follow in the same road. If it absolutely abandons the old methods and adopts the new, then we Socialists should join it; but until then our duty is to reason with it, and try to show it how mistaken it is, but otherwise to treat it as we would any other party engaged in the burlesque work carried on at Westminster.

We shall of course be told by the Labour party as we are by other nominal Socialists, who have more than a half belief that Socialism is not necessary since the present system can be so improved as to meet all reasonable requirements, that we are impracticable purists, so bigoted that we would rather do nothing for the workmen than take less than a complete system of Socialism. This is, however, a complete inversion of the facts. It is they who will do nothing that can be of any practical use, and who are delaying serious legislation by leading the workmen who have not given thought to the subject on the road of palliative measures which they would know if they were really Socialists will take them out of the only road that can lead to economic well-being. Like Christian in the Pilgrim's Progress, they see the road lying straight before them to be rough and difficult, while the bye-path of palliatives is smooth and easy, and not having perfect faith in the guide who had told them the right road to take, they take the apparently easy one which, however, brings them no nearer to the heavenly city. Those who are true Socialists and who know that Socialism alone can benefit the workmen will not follow on the wrong road, but will endeavour to persuade the workmen to join them in taking the right.

Palliative measures are, one and all, delusive; each of them bringing as much loss to the working classes as gain; and, perhaps, even more. The utmost that can be said for the best of them is that a temporary advantage is obtained while the corresponding disadvantage may perhaps come only at a later time. There are many changes proposed by the Radicals, and now, I believe, by the Labour party, which are absolutely unimportant as far as the working classes are concerned, but which, in spite of the clearest teaching of experience that they are worthless, are still put forward as part of the programme by which economic well-being is to be obtained. Chief among these is the nationalisation of land, railways, tramways, &c., and we will discuss this subject somewhat at length, mainly because this sort of work has a specious appearance of being Socialistic, at least in its tendency. Since Socialism proposes to nationalise all the implements of production, it is argued that the nationalisation of some of them must be at least a step towards Socialism. This is not, however, the case. It is a strange kind of Socialism which national-ises the implements of one class of capitalists for the sole benefit of another, and this is all that would happen were part only of the implements of production nationalised. Australia and New Zealand, the great leaders in Radical legislation, have furnished us with examples in point. They have nationalised their railways, tram cars, water works, gas works, &c., and yet they are suffering even more than English workmen from want of employment and poverty. They have even made their experiment scien-tifically complete by leaving a railway here and there un-nationalised, so that we can more clearly see how unim-portant the whole thing is, by seeing that the part of the country served by the unnationalised railway is neither better nor worse off than the part served by the national-ised railways. The workmen in Australia have learned by experience that nationalising the railways is not a matter which concerns them, and they are not in the least anxious that all the railways shall be nationalised. It is the capitalists who live along the line who are interested in the matter. They want the unnationalised railways to be nationalised, because they know that they will get their transport cheaper, the difference in cost being made good by taxation levied from others.

The first question that arises in discussing this matter is whether you are going to pay for the railways which you nationalise? If you do, you must manage them much as is done at present so that you may get the revenue with which to pay the shareholders; and it is not easy to see what advantage either workmen or other capitalists would gain by the change. If you do not pay for them you are simply taxing the shareholders to the extent of their entire incomes, while leaving all other capitalists untaxed. Having done this, you could afford to run cheap trains, but this would only be transferring to those who use the railways the income the shareholders formerly enjoyed, and would do no sort of good to the working classes.

The Radicals, however, say the working classes would really gain by the change. Their masters would get so large an addition to their profits that they could afford to pay higher wages to the men, and would therefore do so, the shareholders' profits being thus really transferred to the workmen. This argument is the foundation of not only Radical but also of Tory legislation, the "protection to native industry" advocated by both parties having it as its ground-work. What does the argument really amount to? The capitalists, including landlords, make a profit of about £1,000,000,000 a year, and it is seriously contended that they cannot out of this pittance pay their men higher wages. If, however, the railway shareholders were looted and their profits transferred to other capitalists the latter could then, it is contended, afford to pay higher wages. It really is strange that men who claim to be thinking statesmen can seriously use such arguments. The capital-ists get £1,000,000,000 a year solely because the working classes take no proper steps to prevent them from getting it, and until these steps are taken anything deducted from profits of one class will not come to the workmen, but will join the rest of the £1,000,000,000, and go into the pockets of another class of capitalists.

Again it is said that the Government would manage the railways better than the companies do, and I think myself this would be the case. We have, however, overwhelming evidence to show that the well-being of the workmen does not in the least depend on the good or bad management of capitalists, not on the efficiency or inefficiency of labour. Six hundred years ago labour in England was wretchedly inefficient. One modern workman using steam looms and steam ploughs and threshing machines will produce as much as a whole village of his forefathers, and yet he is no better off than his forefathers were. The whole increase in the efficiency of labour has gone to benefit the capitalists, and any increase that may be obtained in the future, whether from nationalising railways or otherwise, will go the same road. In the face of a fact like this, is it not the veriest childishness to endeavour to benefit the working classes by the wretched huckstering policy now popular, of throwing obstacles in the way of foreign competition? If you can keep foreigners from competing with native capitalists, you may perhaps increase the profits of the native capitalists, but what possible interests have the working classes in raising the profits of capital from £1,000,000,000 to £1,001,000,000? The workmen will not get a penny of the odd million, as is amply proved by the fact that they have not got a penny of the £990,000,000 that have been added to capitalists' yearly profits during the last six hundred years.

For the same reason the working classes have no interest in the economies or extravagances of the Chancellor of the Exchequer. If he is economical, so much the better for capitalists; but the workmen have no interest in the matter, since none of the savings will go permanently to them. A change in the method of collecting taxes may temporarily affect them it is true. Were, for instance, the duties on tea and tobacco removed, workmen would gain to that extent; but the saving would be almost at once either deducted from their wages or added to their rents. The removal of all taxation would be equivalent to increasing the efficiency of labour by ten or twelve per cent.; but increased efficiency, although important to capitalists, is not of importance to workmen, since the

greater product obtained goes to the masters and not to
the men.

The whole mechanism of the political economy of a
capitalist society has been, in short, framed and designed
for the purpose of enabling those who own the world and
all that it contains to get as much as possible out of those
who do not share in this vast property. It is admirably
adapted to that work; but from the very nature of its con-
struction it cannot be patched and mended so as to make it
work for the benefit of the very people it was designed to
exploit. Their only chance of improvement lies in abolishing the system; and there is absolutely nothing to prevent
this being done to-morrow except the ignorance of the
workmen on the subject, and the idea, which defenders of
capitalism are careful to keep alive, that there would be
great difficulty in making the change. Wherein, however,
does the difficulty consist? If every workshop in the
country continued to produce what it is now producing,
we should have the same yearly product as we now have,
and surely it is not an impossible problem to arrange for
a fair distribution of the goods. Provided the goods are
produced, the problem of sub-dividing them is comparatively simple; and they will be produced if the factories
of the country are all kept at work. The only legal
machinery required to effect the change would be a short
Act of Parliament declaring all property to be nationalised;
and perhaps devolving on the Parish Councils, as a
temporary measure, the duty of seeing that all the factories
in the Parish were kept at work.

The industry of a country like England is of course
extremely complex and involved, and goods in an incom-
plete form have to pass through a hundred factories in the
course of production. In order that this may be done in a
regular and efficient manner, an elaborate system of
accounts, corresponding to the finance of commerce, would
be required. We have not, however, to invent such a
system, for it is already invented for us, and we have only
to modify to a very slight extent the existing system in
order to do the same work that the capitalists now do so
easily. At present we have in the capitalist a hereditary
and despotic master, who by the help of a complex system
of finance is enabled to send the goods he produces without
difficulty to the point where they are required. The
Socialist master would be a constitutional monarch elected

by his comrades; but he could do the same work that the despotic master now does as easily as an elected president does the political work of an hereditary emperor.

It would undoubtedly take a few years to learn the new system of accounts, and during the period of transition it is quite certain that labour will not be applied in the best manner. We have, however, a very wide margin to cover any errors of management. Our forefathers at least lived, and they even lived comfortably, although they knew nothing of the steam engine, and surely we, with the steam engine, can live as well as they did, even though we bungle a good deal in our management. Nine men out of every ten are now employed in producing useless goods, which add nothing to the comfort and well-being of man; but are merely tokens to show that those who buy them are wealthy and not mere common clay. It is not easy to change a man's work; but a great many of these men and all their children could be turned to better employments, while the implements with which all of them work would form the raw material for creating useful implements.

For a few years there would be confusion and mismanagement; for a few months there might even be privation, although not a fiftieth part as much as the miners underwent in their great strike. In a very short time, however, the new system of economic management would be learnt, goods would pass from hand to hand as readily and as regularly under an elected, as they now do under a hereditary chief, labour would flow as readily to the occupations most conducive to the well-being of the workers as it now flows to those the capitalists think most conducive to their well-being, and the efficiency of labour would be so great that one twentieth of the population could supply themselves and the rest with all the necessaries of life, the other nineteen-twentieths being employed in producing whatever goods were preferred.

It must not be supposed that the Socialist economic mechanism would require, as our opponents always assume, a vast horde of professional organisers, or that we should have ministers analogous to the Postmaster-General to superintend every branch of industry. The work to be done under Socialism is precisely the same as is required under capitalism, and professional organisers are no more wanted in the one case than in the other. There are in England hundreds of thousands of separate

and distinct factories all of which are necessary to the
work of each other. In order that they may be kept at
work goods of all kinds have to be passed backwards and
forwards from one to the other in an almost infinitely
complex maze; but there are no organisers to instruct the
capitalists as to when and whither their goods shall be
sent. The capitalists have invented a system of finance
which, although complex, is sufficiently simple to be practically worked, and which fully instructs everyone as to
the best manner of managing his factory. A very similar,
although greatly simpler, finance would in the same way
instruct the elected manager of a Socialist factory how he
should manage it, and he would have no more need for
advice from a professional organiser than a capitalist has.

Nor would a Socialist State require a more intellectual
or a more moral class of rulers or workers than a capitalist
state, although a higher morality than now exists would
certainly arise. Under the present system the earth is the
capitalists', and the fullness thereof; and those who come
into the world without any share in its ownership cannot
but be serfs to those who own it. To upset so absurd a
system would only be the exercise of common sense on the
part of those who suffer under it; and it is not necessary
that they shall be men of special moral or intellectual
qualities. Having once obtained their economic freedom,
surely no overwhelming genius is needed to show them
that if they won't work neither can they eat. Nor does it
require high moral qualities in those who work to insist
that everyone shall do his fair share of the work, under
penalty of not getting any share of what is produced. At
the same time there will assuredly be a great change in
the attitude of the society as a whole towards what may be
called the unsocialist or criminal classes. A dislike of
work is as much a disease as small-pox, and one who
would not work would be sent rather to the physician than
to the jailor.

The A B C *of* SOCIALISM

by FRED HENDERSON

TWOPENCE

INDEPENDENT LABOUR PARTY
PUBLICATION DEPARTMENT
14 GREAT GEORGE ST., WESTMINSTER

This pamphlet is the first chapter of "The Case for Socialism," in which book other chapters deal with SOCIALISM AND

CONFISCATION
PERSONAL PROPERTY
LIBERTY
OFFICIALISM
UNEMPLOYMENT
WASTE
LEVELLING DOWN
HUMAN NATURE

144 *pages, paper covers, One Shilling; cloth covers 2/6, from all Booksellers and I.L.P. Publication Department, 14 Great George Street, Westminster, London. S.W.1.*

The A B C *of* Socialism

NOBODY can exercise the rights of citizenship intelligently nowadays without clearly understanding the case for Socialism. At parliamentary and municipal elections, in every department of public affairs, the issues are defined, with constantly increasing insistence, in terms of Socialism and Anti-Socialism ; not only in the direct proposals put forward by Socialists themselves, but in the implications of the Socialist idea in the proposals of all political parties. And no vote can be an intelligent vote unless there is behind it a knowledge of the Socialist case and a reasoned judgment upon the Socialist idea.

The Socialist movement has passed beyond that ordeal stage which every new movement has to encounter, the stage of mere unreasoning prejudice and the unstudied use of epithets against it. Within the life of a single generation it has drawn to its ranks millions of earnest thinking men and women ; and it has made out its case so convincingly that in every civilised country its capture of the power of government is now the dominant issue in political conflict. It is sweeping on from strength to strength ; challenging the old order everywhere with confident boldness. Here in Great Britain its hands are already on the reins of government ; and there is manifest in the utterances of its opponents a bewildered sense of the futility of their efforts to stay its march to power. It claims to explain to the common man why poverty and squalor exist in a world of abundant resources ; and the common man is everywhere finding in it the hope of fulfilment for his dream of human life set free from these miseries. In these circumstances, every citizen who wishes to keep intelligently abreast of the responsibilities of his citizenship must study the Socialist case ; and the desire amongst reasonable people for a serious study and understanding of it is now everywhere manifest. It is to meet this desire, to provide a statement of the essential teaching of Socialism, that this book is written.

In the first place, we Socialists believe that poverty can be prevented. The fact we ask you to begin by bearing in mind is that people are not poor in Great Britain because Great Britain is a poor country. We believe that the civilized world is able to produce enough wealth to give a high standard of life to all its people, if only that wealth could be got into the lives of its people.

Our first point, therefore, is that poverty is not inevitable ; that the resources of the world are sufficient to prevent it ; and that it could be prevented if only the nation saw clearly what it is that stops the wealth of the country from getting into the homes of the people and being available for the general life.

That may seem like a commonplace to you. But if you will think about it for a moment, you will see that it establishes a very real difference between Socialism and all other political ideas.

All other parties take the fact of poverty for granted, as being part of the natural and inevitable order of human affairs.

It is true that both Liberals and Conservatives put forward schemes of social reform intended to get rid of the extremes of poverty ; such schemes as those for old-age pensions, for feeding necessitous school children, for ensuring workmen against unemployment, and the like. That is all good so far as it goes ; but it does not touch the actual problem of the cause of poverty. On the contrary, it assumes that there will continue to be poverty to be relieved in these ways. These reforms are only proposals for giving

relief ; and amount to no more than constantly baling out
the boat while the leak which causes all the trouble is left
untouched. The problem of poverty can only be effectively
dealt with at its source—by stopping the leak.

What both Liberals and Conservatives take for granted
is the broad fact of a rich class and a poor class continuing
to exist ; a population on the one hand living at ease with
all the comforts of a spacious life, and a working population
on the other hand living in small houses, with little leisure,
and with incomes only at or about the margin of subsistence.

No political party other than the Socialist party has any
idea of fundamentally altering that state of things. They
are quite willing to give us reforms within the existing
social order ; and would be glad to see the poor class
assured of regular work and wages good enough to go a
little beyond the bare margin of subsistence ; so that, for
instance, working men might live in suburban streets of
artisans' houses instead of in slums, have a little back
garden to cultivate, work eight hours a day instead of ten
or twelve, and even get a week or a fortnight for holiday
in the summer.* But the broad fact of a rich class and a
poor class would remain ; a small rich class with spacious
lives and a large poor class with comparatively little. The
notion of the other political parties is that practical politics
are limited to such reforms as simply mitigate the extremes
of poverty ; the Socialist idea is that the national resources
should be made available for the general national life, and
that this class division, being in itself an evil and unjust
thing, should cease.

When therefore, we Socialists say that poverty can be
prevented, you will see that we mean by " poverty "

* In precisely the same way, while serfdom existed there were
all sorts of proposals put forward by humane people for relaxing
the conditions of serfdom, making it less intolerable for the serf,
while still retaining the institution of serfdom as part of the social
order. What was wrong, of course, was not that the conditions
of serfdom were too harsh and required to be modified, but that
the institution of serfdom itself was unjust, and required to be
abolished. The position with regard to private capitalism is
precisely the same in relation to all this proposed reform within
the existing order.

something very different from utter destitution. Poverty
is not an absolute term. It is a relative term ; relative
to the kind of life which the actual resources of the world
might make possible for men.

A man is a poor man if he is shut out from any of the
possibilities of human life within the range of the general
existing resources of the world.

He may have his animal wants supplied ; may have a
sufficiency of food, of clothing, and of shelter. His
master's cattle have that, according to their cattle standard.
But that is not human life. If the resources of the world
are ample—as they are ample—to provide for all men leisure
and a high standard of the graces of life as well as of its
animal satisfactions, he is a poor man so long as he is shut
out from the full enjoyment of those graces. We Socialists
refuse to accept as an adequate standard of life any standard
which stops short of full human life. The habit of setting
up separate class standards as to what is an adequate kind
of life is so engrained in the minds of men to-day that it is
the commonest thing to hear rich men denouncing as
extravagant and unreasonable any claim by working men
to many things which the employer class would find an
intolerable deprivation in having to go without themselves.
We Socialists present our challenge straight in the face of
that class idea. We say that a man is a man, and that we
will have no class standards in these things.

We set up a human standard. And whatever kind of
life the general resources of the world can make possible
for all men has to go into that standard ; and as the powers
of men over Nature increase, and their wealth producing
activities become more and more fruitful by reason of
growing knowledge and invention, that increase has got
to go into the general standard, raising the general level of
life, leaving no class out of the general advance.

To be below that standard is to be poor. To reserve
for the enjoyment of a class alone any of these things which
might be the common human heritage is evidence of
injustice in our social organisation. And if the whole of
the proposals of the orthodox political parties for " social
reform " within the existing order were carried out to-

morrow, this fundamental injustice of class division and class privilege would still remain.

We should still not have a human society ; but a class society of the rich and an underworld of the poor.

You see, therefore, something of what we Socialists mean when we say that our aim is to make the national resources available for the general life of the nation.

The question is : How can it be done ?

And you cannot answer that question until you first see clearly what it is that now prevents the resources of the nation from getting into the life of the nation. To that point, therefore, our enquiry must in the first place be carefully directed.

The wealth upon which the world lives is produced by labour, skill, and thought, working upon land and capital.

Now, look at the two classes into which society is broadly divided, and you will see that they get their shares of that wealth in different ways.

The class which gives the labour, skill, and thought, lives upon wages.

The class which owns the land and capital lives upon rent, interest, and profit.

*In both cases the livelihood comes out of the current daily wealth production of the world.**

And broadly speaking, the method of getting one's living by wages represents the bare life, and the people who get their living in that way are the poor class ; while the method of getting one's living by rent, interest, and profit represents the full life, and the people who get their living in that way are the rich class.

There are exceptions, of course. There are people living poorly upon rents and dividends, and highly skilled experts living well upon wages. There is a certain mixture of classes. You do not have a mass of poor people living on wages, then a gap, and on the other side of the gap a

* Note this very carefully ; you will see its importance as the argument develops.

mass of rich people living upon rent and dividends. From abject poverty to great wealth there is every sort of gradation in between. Some small owners supplement their little rents or dividends by earning wages, and some wage-earners save a little and draw dividends on a small scale. But, broadly speaking, the generalization is true that the distinctive way of living of the poor class is by wages, and the distinctive way of living of the rich class is by ownership.

The purpose of our enquiry, therefore, is to discover how it is that the resources of the nation, daily produced by the activities of the nation, should be distributed in this way. Why is it that ownership should mean one way of life and industry another way of life ; the one spacious, the other poor ?

And here a brief digression is necessary in order to make every step in the argument perfectly clear as we go along ; a digression of which the reader will find the germ in the footnote to the previous paragraph calling upon him to note specially the fact that " in both cases the livelihood comes out of the current daily wealth production of the world."

The facts as to this must be made as clear as possible.

The problem into which we are enquiring is not a problem of one class possessing resources and the other not. It is a problem of the distribution day by day of the resources *which are being produced day by day by the industry of the world.*

It is upon this point that most confusion exists in the minds of those who do not think clearly on these matters. They imagine the rich man possessing wealth and living upon that wealth, inheriting it from his father, paying wages out of it to the people he employs, and so on. Nothing of the sort. *The whole nation, rich and poor, lives upon the current daily wealth production of the world.*

The rich man owns land. But he does not live on land. He lives on wealth produced out of the land by industry. He owns capital. But he does not live on capital. He lives on wealth produced day by day by industry applied to his capital. The whole worth of his land and capital as a means of income to him is in the industry attached to that land and capital, and in the constant production of that industry. He does not pay wages to anyone. The industry produces its own wages as well as his income. If any workman doubts that, let him ask himself whether he would be allowed to stop ten minutes in the factory if he did *not* produce his own wages and something over.

The rich man does not inherit the wealth upon which he lives. He cannot live upon any form of wealth other than the wealth which is being produced round about him day by day. What he inherits is *power over the sources of that wealth.* Land is the primary source of all wealth. Labour applied to land makes it fruitful ; and it is upon that perishable and constantly renewed fruitfulness that the world lives. It is fruitful, not in food only, but in its minerals, its timber, its products out of which invention and labour shape the implements of the more complicated wealth production of modern life. As civilization advances, the production of these implements becomes greater and greater, representing vast powers of creating wealth when human energy and human ingenuity works with and upon them.

It is power over these sources of production, land and capital, which the rich man inherits ; and the value of that inheritance is that it is a means of making the immediate perishable wealth upon which the world lives flow into his life as fast as it is produced.

You will thus see that, when you speak about the distribution of our national wealth, it is necessary to guard very carefully against the common error of picturing to yourself that wealth as a sort of fixed and permanent thing. When, for example, people repeat the familiar idiotcy which some of the more stupid amongst them imagine to be an argument against Socialism, that if you divided up all the wealth of the country to-day there would be inequalities again to-morrow, the simple-minded error into which they fall is that of supposing the wealth of the country to be a fixed and permanent thing, which you could get together into a heap and divide up. You could, of course, do nothing of the kind, even if anybody were silly enough to suggest it.

The problem of the distribution of wealth is not the problem of an act of distribution, but of a continuous process of distribution. The wealth of the country is a constantly produced, constantly distributed, constantly consumed stream of commodities ; and the problem of its distribution is not a problem of its division at any given moment, but a problem *of having proper channels for its constant and regular flow into the life of the nation.*

I have put this point at some length because a thorough grasp of it is of fundamental importance. Confusion of mind about it means confused and fallacious thinking on the whole economic problem. Clearly see this true nature of the wealth on which the world lives—how it is in constant production and constant consumption, how it is created and used and done with day by day—and the problem of its distribution at once presents itself to you in a clearer light. The error into which people fall is that of supposing that the rich class actually possess great wealth, and that the Socialists wish to take it from them and give it to the mass of the people. Whereas, I repeat again, the fact is that what the rich possess is power to divert from the mass of the people the flow of the wealth which the labour of the mass of the people constantly produces ; so that wealth which does not now exist at all, wealth which will be created to-morrow, next week, next year, counts as their possession, and will flow into their lives steadily and constantly as fast as it is produced.

It is this process of distribution which is the important thing.

The rich class possess wealth which is now passing through the national life ; but that is only incidental to their power over the sources of wealth and over the process of its production and distribution. The real nature of their class privilege is that they possess the power of appropriating wealth which is or will be created at any time, now, hereafter, and to all time if the existing system continues.

And so we get back to the question on which this digression arose : What is it that prevents the resources of the nation from getting into the life of the nation ? How is it that this constantly flowing stream of wealth, flowing from the daily activities of the nation, how is it that, instead of irrigating the whole life of the nation, it runs in such a way as to make a few lives grow rank with excessive luxury, and leaves myriads of other lives bleak and dry ?

Is not the answer to that question already becoming clear to you ? Hark back for a moment to what we saw is the fundamental distinction between the two classes, and the different ways in which they get their living. The distinctive way of living of the poor class is by wages ; the distinctive way of living of the rich is by rent, interest, and profits. Evidently the difference between incomes derived from wages and incomes derived from rent, interest, and profits, gives us the clue to be followed up in this enquiry as to what it is that prevents the resources of the nation from getting into the general life of the nation.

The best way of following up that clue is to take an actual case of wealth production under normal capitalist conditions, and see what happens.

Here, for instance, is a boot factory where a thousand men (they are largely women and boys, to be strictly accurate) are engaged in producing boots and shoes. By the end of the week, labour, operating upon capital in the form of raw material and machinery, has created new wealth in the form of finished boots and shoes.

The value of the finished boots and shoes includes the value of the raw material and the industry of a vast army of people engaged in preparing that material, from the cattle-tender to the tanner, before it comes into the hands of the shoe operative at all ; beside the industry and skill of those who, from inventor to miner, have placed at the disposal of the operative the machinery with which he works. But the shoe operative by transforming this raw material into the finished article, has created a new value and brought new wealth into existence, value and wealth which is his human energy embodied in the boots and shoes.

How is that new wealth distributed ?

The whole of it belongs to the man who owns the factory.

At the end of the week, having come into possession of this newly created wealth, the owner pays a portion of its value back to the operative in the form of wages.

What is it that regulates the amount so paid back as wages ?

Just in the same way as oil and fuel have to be supplied to the inanimate machinery to keep it in a state of working efficiency, so the workman, the human machinery, has to be supplied with food and clothes and shelter to keep him in efficient working order. The owner of the factory buys labour as cheaply as he can. Wages represent the cost of keeping labour alive and working,—the cost of running the human machinery of the factory.

Now compare this with the position of the slave under a slave-owner. When the slave-owner bought a man, he bought labour. The value of the slave to his owner was the slave's capacity for labour. All that the slave produced belonged to his owner. The cost of the slave's keep had to come out of it ; and the owner lived upon the surplus.

So far as the distribution of wealth between the slave-owner and the slave is concerned, is it not analogous to the distribution of wealth between ownership and industry under capitalism ?

The slave-owner had to make three payments—the payment of a lump sum down for the slave, the payment for land and tools and equipment for the slave to work with, and after that the constant daily payment of the cost of the slave's maintenance.

The capitalist has this advantage over the slave-owner, that he escapes the first of these payments. He gets his labour for nothing, and calls that process " providing men with employment," claiming to be a benefactor to the community by doing so. All they produce belongs to him, in exactly the same way that all the slave produced belonged to the slave-owner. The cost of their keep has to come out of it in the form of wages and the owner takes the surplus.

That is the process by which the constantly produced wealth of the country is distributed between wages on the one hand, and rent, interest, and profit on the other. We Socialists can see no essential difference between this system, which we call " wage slavery " and the old system of chattel slavery. There are superficial and non-essential differences in detail ; but the two things are identical in the main fact that the slave-owner and the capitalist both live in exactly the same way—upon the surplus wealth remaining after paying the cost of maintenance of the labour which produces that wealth.

The chief superficial difference between the two forms of slavery is that whereas the slave-owner owned both the man and the means of the man's work, the capitalist owns only the means of the man's work. Under this latter system the man is nominally free. But in its practical consequences there is little real difference between owning the man and owning the means of the man's work. The man is helpless without access to the means of his work. He must either sell himself into wage slavery to the owner of the means of his work, or starve. It comes to the same practical end in either case ; whether you own the man or only own the means of his work, either form of ownership gives you power to take possession of everything the man produces, simply for the price of his keep out of it.

We come, therefore, to the fact of private ownership and control of the means of the nation's work, as the explanation of the present one-sided distribution of the national wealth ; the reason why vast armies of people live in poverty in a land of plenty. The nation's industry is carried on for the profit of its proprietors, and society is organised for their exclusive benefit. The share which the workman gets is simply maintenance for himself and his family, necessary to keep wealth production going. It is not regarded by the employing class as being really 'part of the national distribution of wealth at all. The industry of the nation belongs to them ; and they look upon the amount paid in wages simply as a charge upon their resources ; a charge which they enter in their accounts as " cost of labour " ; so much taken off the profits ; an expense in the same category as the expense of machinery or fuel. The workman has no status, no right to work or to live, unless they find it profitable to employ him. He is an alien in the land, taking his place in organised society only by permission of an owner and on condition of being able to find a proprietor willing to buy him. What is spent upon his keep is, from the point of view of his proprietor, merely one of the expenses of business to be set against the profit got out of his labour ; like the cost of feeding cattle set against the price of beef.

We can now see pretty clearly how it is that the constantly produced stream of national wealth is distributed ; and why it is that the distinctive fact about poverty is that men live by wages, while the distinctive fact about the spacious kind of life is that men live by ownership. The private ownership of land and capital stands revealed as simply a device for enabling a small class to live by imposing their maintenance upon the industry of the community ; diverting into their possession, as fast as it it produced, the whole of the wealth created by the national industry over and above the necessary maintenance of the workers.

Ask yourself, frankly, is that way of living honest ?
We Socialists assert that there is no moral difference between this process of capitalist exploitation of the workers and ordinary pocket-picking or brigandage. To us, the gentleman class which lives in this way is merely a class of " disgraceful sponging creatures." I put this general consideration of the ethics of the question to you,—that in a world in which no human need is served without human industry, there must be a process of dishonesty hidden somewhere in the social and industrial arrangements which send the flow of the world's wealth into non-productive lives. Call it what fine names you please—rent or interest or return on capital or unearned increment—the fact remains that in its essential character it is theft, tribute levied by an idle class upon industry.

" Oh, but," you say, " it is legal. After all, the land and capital belong to these people ; and surely they have a right to their income from it."

To which I reply that it is this private ownership of land and capital which we Socialists indict as the root cause of poverty. We challenge its justice and its right to exist or continue. We trace directly to it the ruin, the widespread misery and destitution, of the mass of the people.

In the first place, we point out to you that the proprietor class get their capital in exactly the same way as they get their income,—out of the surplus produced by industry over and above the cost of maintaining those engaged in the industry. Capital is no more a fixed and permanent thing than is the currently consumed wealth on which the world lives. Like that wealth, capital is constantly being used up and constantly being renewed by fresh production. I have before me as I write the half-yearly statement of accounts and balance sheet of one of our great railway companies. I find in it, as I find in it every half-year, a heavy item of expense set down for depreciation and renewals. What does that mean ? It means that during the half-year a certain proportion of the capital of the company has been used up, worn out of existence ; and that it is being renewed and replaced out of the half-year's revenue. And that happens every half-year. Within a sufficient period of years, a comparatively short period, practically the whole of the capital of the company is worn up and wiped out of existence, and replaced out of revenue in this way. And so it is with every business undertaking. It provides its own capital as it goes along. The capital upon which labour is now operating in my neighbour's boot factory is capital provided by labour, capital provided out of the revenue of the business as the business has grown and developed. That is what is meant by " a developing business " ; a business whose capital is obtained out of revenue, not only for replacing that which is constantly wearing out—the business would become bankrupt if it did not do that—but also for extending and enlarging it. The whole thing comes out of labour, the capital as well as the profits.

As for landownership,—well, it is hardly necessary nowadays to be a Socialist to see what most Liberals and many orthodox politicians admit, that there is, and there can be, no moral or just title whatever to the private ownership of land.

Land is the primary need of the human race. It is the essential thing ; the storehouse from which, in the first instance, we draw all our resources. Human life depends absolutely upon it, as absolutely as upon the air we breathe. The land of the country is the nation's birthright and means of existence, upon the use and occupation of which all our activities depend, and without which life itself is impossible.

To have private persons in the position of being able to demand toll and tribute for the use of the earth, the natural creation, is against public policy. It is a violation of the common right of the human race. It is the enslavement of the nation.

It is legal, no doubt. But so was slavery. So was serfdom. Its legality simply comes down to us from the time when our institutions were whatever the lords and masters of the world were able, by force or fraud, to set up for their own advantage. It belongs to the category of the many devices by which servitude has been fastened upon the peoples of the earth. Trace the title to land back, and always the original title is the title of force, of the sword, of the armed robber powerful enough to establish his lordship over other men or cunning enough to alienate the patrimony of his clan to himself. No moral validity whatever attaches to this device of placing the people under permanent tribute to the robber class for ever and ever by giving legal sanction (legal sanction in this matter meaning the sanction of the robbers themselves, who controlled law making) to private ownership of the thing essential to life.

That is the meaning of private landownership. When you say that a man owns land, you are simply describing a state of things by which one man possesses the power of taxing for his own benefit all the life and industry over a given area ; making the whole population pay him tribute for the right to live in their native land. You might just as well have air-ownership ; rent-charges for the right to breathe. That would be in no way more ridiculous than the claim to private landownership. The whole thing is merely a device for imposing the maintenance of an idle class upon the labour of the countryside, compelling the people who live and work upon the land to maintain a powerful group of brigands ; and is happily ceasing to be regarded as respectable even amongst orthodox politicians.

The position occupied by the landowning and industry-owning class can be best illustrated by a comparison. Up till a little over a hundred years ago we had in England what was known as " the sinecure system." It was a beautiful arrangement of Providence for providing incomes for the younger sons and poor relations of the governing classes. Nearly every post in the public service of this country was filled by the appointment of a " Place holder." He was appointed under Letters Patent by the Crown at an adequate salary, with leave to appoint a deputy. The word " Placeholder " conveys to us to-day nothing of its old official meaning. When we speak of a placeholder to-day, we simply mean a man who holds an office of some sort or other ; though a sufficient reminiscence of its earlier meaning still clings to the word to give it, so far as it is now used at all, an implication of easy office. But under the old system it did not mean a man who held an office in any responsible sense at all. It merely meant a man who owned an estate in the emoluments of an office with the work of which he had nothing to do. The estate in the office and the actual work in the office were as separate and distinct as an estate in land and actual work on the land are separate and distinct to-day. The estate in the office was simply a means of drawing emoluments from the work of the office, exactly as an estate in land is a means of drawing tribute from industry on the land. The whole system of Patent Placeholding was a device for quartering favoured people on the public purse. The younger son or the poor relation of this or that governing family was given the Place. His Letters Patent were his title deeds. Not infrequently the Place was inherited, like any landed estate.

The person holding it appointed a deputy at a small remuneration, and lived on the rest of the income of his Place and its emoluments, without having any duties whatever to perform. At the beginning of the eighteenth century, practically the whole public service of this country was estated in this way to " Patent Placeholders " ;   and the nation had the honour of maintaining by this device the otherwise unprovided-for members of the governing classes.

For example, George Selwyn, famous as a wit and a man about town, was a Placeholder. He was " Clerk of the Irons and Surveyor of the Melting Houses in the Tower of London." " Paymaster of the works concerning the repairs and well-keeping of His Majesty's Houses," " Surveyor General of Crown Lands," " Clerk of the Crown and Peace, and Registrar of the Court of Chancery in the Island of Barbadoes "—it was the Court, says his biographer with sly humour, " it was the Court which was in the Barbadoes, and not the Registrar "—and so on. These Places were, of course, absolute sinecures. The Placeholder simply drew an income from them ; and the whole civil service, by being allocated in estates in this way, was made a means of providing a settlement in life for an army of idle and irresponsible persons ; exactly as the land is now.

In 1782 Burke abolished most of these sinecures. And exactly the same cry about " confiscation and robbery " and " depriving people of their property," which is now raised by landowners and capitalists against Socialism, was raised by the Patent Placeholders. Horace Walpole, himself a Placeholder several times over, wrote very bitterly about it.

" He who holds an ancient Patent Place," he said," enjoys it as much by law as any gentleman holds his estate ; and from the same fountain, by grants from the Crown, as I possess my Places."

And Horace Walpole was perfectly right. There is no difference whatever between landownership and the old system of Patent Placeholding. They are both nothing more or less than devices for imposing the maintenance of a parasite class upon the resources of the nation.*

Socialism puts it to you that the settlement of this problem of poverty can only be brought about by getting rid of the Placeholders who are bleeding the life of the country white by the tribute-levying system of private ownership of the land and capital of the country. The nation, if it desires its resources to get into the homes and lives of its people, must own its own land and capital, and so control the sources of the wealth upon which it lives ; must organise its own industry, and carry on the production of the national wealth for use in the general national life.

That is Socialism : Community ownership of the land and of the means of producing and distributing wealth ; and the organisation of industry under that common ownership as public service for the benefit of all ; directed to social ends and the equipment of the life of the whole people instead of, as now, to the private enrichment of a privileged class of owners.

That is what Socialists are working for. The Socialist party cannot do it, and does not pretend to be able to do it. The nation must do it. Socialism is not something that the Socialists say they are going to do for you. It is a principle of national life and organisation, which the nation must adopt or reject for itself. Our mission in politics is to convince you of the justice of this principle. We believe that in this proposal lies the hope of the world, the possibility of a real human society in which citizenship shall be—as citizenship in a civilized community should be —the guarantee given by the collective life of the nation of full opportunity to every man and woman.

The enslavement of men by their fellow men has taken many forms in human history. Whatever its form may

* It is worth noting, in passing, as an illustration of how history repeats itself, that one of the arguments used on behalf of the Placeholders was that by their expenditure they provided a great deal of employment for the poor ; and that the abolition of these Patent Places would therefore be a very serious injury to the working-man !

be, the substance and reality of enslavement is that it gives one man the power to say to other men, " I shall live pleasantly on the good things of the world by making you provide them for me." Whatever the device may be which enables men to do that, is slavery, The fight against private ownership of land and capital, the fight for Socialism, for the nation's control of its own resources, is the last fight in the age-long struggle of humanity for freedom ; a struggle which can have but one end. And that end is the final disappearance from human society of the right of an owning class to live by tribute upon the labour of a subject class.

Write to the Head Office of the Independent Labour Party, 14 Great George Street, Westminster, London, S.W.1, for particulars of the work of the Party, and how you may join it. A list of interesting Pamphlets and Books on Socialism and Labour Questions will be sent post free, together with a copy of the Labour Bookshelf, on application to the Manager, Publication Department, at the same address.

The Blackfriars Press, Ltd., 17-23 Albion Street, Leicester—19570

THE WILLIAM MORRIS SOCIETY

The life, work and ideas of William Morris are as important today as they were in his lifetime. *The William Morris Society* exists to make them as widely known as possible.

The many-sidedness of Morris and the variety of his activities bring together in the *Society* those who are interested in him as designer, craftsman, businessman, poet, socialist, or who admire his robust and generous personality, his creative energy and courage. Morris aimed for a state of affairs in which all might enjoy the potential richness of human life. His thought on how we might live, on creative work, leisure and machinery, on ecology and conservation, on the place of the arts in our lives and their relation to politics, as on much else, remains as challenging now as it was a century ago. He provides a focus for those who deplore the progressive dehumanization of the world in the twentieth-century and who believe, with him, that the trend is not inevitable.

The *Society* provides information on topics of interest to its members and arranges lectures, visits, exhibitions and other events. It encourages the reprinting of his works and the continued manufacture of his textile and wallpaper designs. It publishes a journal twice a year, free to members, which carries articles across the field of Morris scholarship. It also publishes a quarterly newsletter giving details of its programme, new publications and other matters of interest concerning

Morris and his circle. Members are invited to contribute items both to the journal and to the newsletter. *The William Morris Society* has a world-wide membership and offers the chance to make contact with fellow Morrisians both in Britain and abroad.

Regular events include a Kelmscott Lecture, a birthday party held in March, and visits to exhibitions and such places as the William Morris Gallery, Red House, Kelmscott Manor and Standen. These visits, our tours and our short residential study courses, enable members living abroad or outside London to participate in the *Society's* activities. The *Society* also has local groups in various parts of Britain and affiliated Societies in the USA and Canada.

For further details, write to:
The Hon. Membership Secretary
Kelmscott House
26 Upper Mall
Hammersmith
London W6 9TA